CELEBRATING A CENTURY

1914-2014

NFTC

NATIONAL FOREIGN TRADE COUNCIL

The NFTC Story
1914 – 2014

By D. Geoffrey Gamble

For the National Foreign Trade Council
And NFTC Foundation

Based on extensive research by
Nathaniel Wiewora

Edited by James Wilkinson, CAE

First published by Dog Ear Publishing
4010 W. 86th Street, Ste H
Indianapolis, IN 46268
www.dogearpublishing.net

dog ear
PUBLISHING

ISBN: 978-1-4575-3412-6

Library of Congress Control Number: has been applied for

This book is printed on acid-free paper.

Printed in the United States of America

Table of Contents

Dedicated to the member companies of the NFTC

Who throughout a century of work

Have stood behind our guiding principles of

Free trade and open markets

For economic growth, job creation,

And a more stable, peaceful world

Acknowledgements

Any project with outsized scope— a full century, in this case—requires many hands to pitch in to help, and many people need to be thanked. If I have omitted anyone here, the fault is my own; please know that the mistake was inadvertant, and accept my earnest and sincere apology.

Our sponsors member companies, and board members listed at the end of this book, for funding the many various elements and events of the NFTC Centennial Celebration of 2014. It has been quite a party!

At the NFTC, for editing drafts of this book and their non-stop work on behalf of NFTC Member Companies and good public policy, Chairman Alan Wolff and President Bill Reinsch;
And the NFTC staff experts: Jake Colvin, Chuck Dittrich, Dan O'Flaherty, Grace O'Rourke, Richard Sawaya, Cathy Schultz, and Bill Sheridan;
For technical and other support, Marshall Lane; as well as Vivian Myers, Sandra Rodriguez, Sarah Frese and Andrew Watrous;
And for laying the groundwork, my predecessor Bill Kelly.

At the Hagley Museum and Library in Wilmington, where the archives of the National Foreign Trade Council, Dr. Roger Horowitz for his gracious hospitality, knowledge and guidance; and Lucas Clawson for his support on site, especially with the Presidential Letters.

Nathaniel Wiewora for wading through 100 years of business meeting minutes and other dusty materials to distill the cruxt of the NFTC.
Donna Rome at One of a Kind Studio for her parallel research efforts for our spectacular 3D commemorative artwork, many of the images appearing also in this book.
Megan Weddle, Amber Ortner, and the team at DogEar Publishing for getting this thing to press on a tight timetable.
And last but not least to Geoff Gamble, for his herculean efforts in getting it done, all while saving the world in his spare time.

—*James Wilkinson*
Washington, DC
2014

PROLOGUE

There would be no American nation without foreign trade. From the end of the 15th century onward, the insatiable demand for gold, spices, and even mandatory fish on Fridays, drove explorers and fishermen to the edge of the earth and back. The New World that awaited them was rich beyond imagining in resources and opportunities. When colonies were planted thick with the adventurous and the discontented from Europe, it was trade - or the prohibition of it in Boston- that sparked the American Revolution. America grew and prospered in the century that followed with canals, with rails of iron, and with the mighty clipper ship trade with what then was known as the Far East. On the American continent, itself, rivers were bridged, mountains were tunneled or blasted away, and, with the advent of automobiles, roads were paved. By the turn of the 20th Century, world trade was more free and unencumbered than it would be for almost a hundred years. The hand of U.S. commerce began to be felt worldwide. At the same time, the United States was coming of age as a world power.

Then came 1914, and things were never the same again. Who would have imagined during that last high summer that the world would darken, and falter, and never really recover, even to this day? The historian Arnold Toynbee, delivering a college commencement address in June of 1964, observed that it was on just such a day that he had been graduated from Oxford fifty years before, and that, a year later, half of his classmates were dead.

In the Spring of 1914, barely three months before the events leading to the Great War spun out of control, something else happened, something good, something that has served not only to stem the chaos and destruction that was the dreadful hallmark of the 20th Century, but to strengthen America as well. The National Foreign Trade Council was conceived.

Since its inception, the NFTC has been the principle voice of American business dedicated to expanding international trade and commerce. At its very first convention, U.S. Steel Chairmen James Farrell, who would lead the NFTC for nearly 50 years, believed that the organization's creation "should become a landmark in the progress of American commerce." Its early members shared a belief that no other issue was as vital to American commerce as ensuring and promoting trade abroad.

For the century since its founding, the NFTC has brought together ever-larger numbers of American exporters and international investors and has remained steadfast in responding to James Farrell's call for American businesses to work together to foster greater prosperity through expanded international commerce and free, fair, and open trade.

—*D. Geoffrey Gamble*
2014

CHAPTER ONE

The Founding of the NFTC:
An Idea Whose Time Had Come

In May 1914, a group of American exporters, shippers, overseas traders, and government officials gathered at the Hotel Raleigh in Washington, DC, to address two interlinked yet long- ignored questions: What problems were Americans trading abroad facing, and how could the United States become the world's pre-eminent global trader[1]? Under the auspices of the first U.S. Secretary of Commerce, William Redfield, several disparate but like-minded associations had organized the meeting: the American Manufacturers' Export Association, the American Asiatic Association, and the Pan-American Society.

Those attending that first National Foreign Trade Convention shared a sense that the second decade of the 20th century was a moment of immense possibility for American trade. By now, the United States had the third-largest volume of foreign trade in the world and possessed an incredible wealth of natural resources. Long-term economic and political developments had made American goods increasingly competitive internationally, and this newfound vigor and competitiveness had led to a recent overseas expansion of American financial institutions and manufacturers. Yet these captains of industry were not satisfied with this position. They believed these fortuitous circumstances obscured less obvious challenges and deeper problems within American trade. Americans who engaged in foreign trade saw no "national foreign trade policy or accepted system of developing foreign trade."[2] Pride and the potential for greater profits, they reasoned, should lead the American business community to fill this void in national leadership. European nations had systematic foreign trade policies that encouraged exporters and protected shipping. The nations of Europe also allowed their domestic firms to work closely abroad in coordinated ways, something American antitrust law prohibited.

In response to this challenge, these traders and investors saw the opportunity to promote an international, expansionist trade worldview. This perspective acquired strength and a public voice through the formation of a growing number of trade associations. These entities sought to overcome business rivalries and press for a common foreign trade agenda. Among these groups were the National Association of Manufacturers, the United States Chamber of Commerce, and the American Manufacturers' Export Association. Together, with the leading manufacturers and shippers of the day, these organizations gathered together under the umbrella of what would come to be called the National Foreign Trade Council.

The Godfather of the National Foreign Trade Council

United States Commerce Secretary William C. Redfield set forth a vision for American trade in speeches and meetings dating to the fall of 1913. Redfield, who held a liberal, expansionist view on trade matters, highlighted the connection between foreign trade and national prosperity. While he pledged that his office would do anything in its power to encourage foreign trade, he emphasized that private enterprise would ultimately have to take the lead. To that end, he proposed a national convention where businessmen from across the nation could gather to discuss the present problems and the future prospects of foreign trade. For this idea Redfield is regarded as the father of the first National Foreign Trade Convention, and thereby, the godfather of the NFTC.[3]

The First Convention: May 27-28, 1914

Heeding Redfield's call, American foreign traders and investors began to organize the first National Foreign Trade Convention. The organizers formed several committees to carry out the planning of the meeting, the sending of invitations, and the preparation of the program. The organizers wanted a largely informational meeting. Businessmen would examine foreign trade from every conceivable angle. They especially wanted speakers who had experience trading or investing abroad. In the eyes of these planners, veterans of global trade could speak uniquely to the difficulties and challenges facing Americans commercially engaged abroad.

Speakers delivered papers in their respective areas of expertise to the convention organizers. These texts were not bromides or homages to American foreign trade; they were instead thoughtful, well-documented pieces focusing on a particular geographic area, problem, or an issue affecting Americans engaged in foreign trade.

The papers were then distributed to the participants well before the beginning of the convention. All delegates were to read these hundreds of pages of material before the convention, so they would be prepared to discuss the authors' ideas during the sessions.

More than 500 people attended the first convention. Delegates represented more than 70 commercial and business organizations. A majority worked for railroad, shipping, or manufacturing companies. One notable attendee was John Francis "Honey Fitz" Fitzgerald, the Mayor of Boston and grandfather of President John Fitzgerald Kennedy, who was there to promote expansion of the Port of Boston. This cross-section of American industry shared an unencumbered, expansionist view of foreign trade. Most also supported increased government support for foreign trade matters. These delegates came from across the nation. Organizers arranged for a special train to bring attendees from New England, New York, Philadelphia, and Baltimore.

Secretary of Commerce William Cox Redfield

William Cox Redfield (1858-1932) was a Democratic politician from New York who became the first Secretary of Commerce in 1913 after the division of the old Department of Commerce and Labor. Redfield began his career working in a post office in Western Massachusetts then moved to a local paper company. After relocating to New York to run a stationery company, he eventually became involved in mining, manufacturing, banking and life insurance. He served as Brooklyn's Commissioner of Public Works before winning a seat in the U.S. House of representatives in a staunchly Republican district. Along the way he authored a book entitled "The New Industrial Day."

With all of the people, papers, and plans in place, the convention opened on May 27, 1914 at the Hotel Raleigh on Pennsylvania Avenue in Washington DC. Alba Johnson, president of Baldwin Locomotive Works, presided over the opening session in the recently remodeled ballroom of this luxurious Beaux Arts hotel. He laid out a series of developments to demonstrate that this moment was a critical one for American exporters, and reminded delegates of the purpose of the convention. Together, they would share ideas as to how American businesses and individuals could trade overseas more productively, leading to greater prosperity for all Americans.

First, Johnson laid out a series of circumstances that made 1914 the perfect year for this meeting. Domestically, the US Government had crafted new institutions and offices in order to promote American trade abroad. The Federal Trade Commission, created in 1914, assisted exporters by collecting information and sharing data about trade and tariffs, and worked with business associations to ensure that cooperation in export trade was executed lawfully. This growing global interest on the part of the government resulted in American firms looking to it for assistance in promoting their overseas ventures. The federal government had begun to pursue a policy of incrementally lowering the nation's tariffs. Lower

The Raleigh Hotel circa 1914

1111 Pennsylvania Avenue NW Washington, DC
Venue of the first National Foreign Trade Convention

tariffs presented both opportunities and complications for American trade. While the policy would inevitably result in more foreign imports, the lower tariff could also open foreign markets to American firms and businesses if the national government insisted upon trade reciprocity.

Abroad, the imminent completion of the Panama Canal could rearrange global commerce, opening up vast new trading possibilities in the Asia Pacific Region by shortening transit times and driving down shipping costs.

Finally, Johnson mentioned the development of a foreign banking capacity. The Federal Reserve Act of 1913 now allowed American banks to establish branches in foreign countries. With Europe in economic recession and teetering on the verge of war, traditional financing modes would be cut off. American banks would therefore have an added incentive to set up branches abroad. The First National City Bank of New York (now Citigroup) was one of the most

Culebra Cut of the Panama Canal, 1914

enthusiastic promoters of overseas commercial banking because of promises from the DuPont Company to conduct its trade through First National's foreign branches. (Citigroup and DuPont, incidentally, remain NFTC Members to this day. Three other firms from the 1914 convention have also remained active NFTC members: Ingersoll-Rand, General Electric, and U.S. Steel.)

Secretary of Commerce Redfield then addressed the Convention, laying out the case for increased foreign trade and what he and his office would do in promotion of the effort:

> "Mr. President and gentlemen of the Convention, this seems to me like getting back into old times again, and it is a particularly happy moment for me because I face a group of men ready and anxious to ride one of my own hobbies.
>
> "I see around me the business warriors who have carried the flag of American industry into many a land...I look with confidence and hope for growth of our foreign trade... I look not only with confidence toward an advance, but to its greatly increased ratio. More than one English and German industrial manager has said to me that the thing he

feared was the awakened mind and the awakened sense of power in American industry.

"I think we are in the midst today of facts which illustrate our competing powers more strongly than they have ever been shown before...The $60,000 per annum (for the Department of Commerce) has become $125,000 for next year...In addition, there has been authorized for the first time the creation of our force of commercial attaches...Men who have had actual experience in foreign trade, and secondly that they speak fluently the language of the country to which they are sent...We have also begun and hope to extend the opening of branch offices of this bureau in New York, Chicago, San Francisco and New Orleans...Five other cities have already petitioned for additional offices of this kind.

"I look to the coming day of our export trade as a day which shall fill us all with pride...Inasmuch as it lies within my power by word of mouth, by official effort and by influence to remove any barriers that may stand in the way of our foreign trade, whether they be at home or abroad, I should think it my privilege and my duty alike to do that."

The next set of speakers highlighted the importance of overcoming business rivalries in promoting American trade abroad. James Farrell, the new president of U.S. Steel Corporation (which Alba Johnson referred to as '*That big brother of American industries*') led this mantra. He remarked that "The nations of the world are no longer, as in earlier times, so largely concerned with military aggrandizement as with commercial prestige." He believed the "first national Convention should become a landmark in the progress of American commerce."[4] In his view, no other issue was as vital to American commerce as ensuring and promoting trade abroad. A systematic policy to encourage foreign trade would stabilize industry. To begin this effort, he suggested creating a body to study the "present trade conditions...in each section of the country, how they can be improved, and what measures will strengthen domestic commerce" as the Germans, English and other European nations had already done. [5] The Committee on Plan and Scope, which he headed, thought it was "proper to consider the commercial conditions of the U.S. and how foreign trade may be affected by legislation in this country and by foreign governments."[6] It believed the convention should consider methods of financing production for foreign trade, the effects of tariff policies, the importance of railway and steamship lines, and how American firms could best cooperate with the government to bolster diplomatic and consular services.

Farrell's call for a standing body of experts to examine these kinds of problems became the National Foreign Trade Council, in the same spirit as the creation of a

James A. Farrell, Founding Chairman of the NFTC

1863-1943

James Augustine Farrell was the President of U.S. Steel from 1911 to 1932. Born in New Haven, Connecticut, his father was a merchant, ship owner, and sea captain from Dublin, Ireland. He took young Farrell on sea journeys, which contributed to his lifelong love of sailing ships. Farrell had begun his career in business as a day laborer at the age of 15, after his father was lost at sea. He entered a wire mill as a laborer and within a few years, he had become an expert wire-drawer. By the time he was 30, Farrell had become the general manager at Pittsburgh Wire. Trouble stuck in 1893, with a severe economic turndown. Drawing on his overseas experience and connections, Farrell decided not to wait the panic out. He aggressively promoted his business abroad and tripled the value of the firm by the end of the century when it was acquired by U.S. Steel. Farrell's experience as a foreign sales agent made him the choice of U.S. Steel to head the foreign development division of the corporation. He rose through the ranks to become president of all of U.S. Steel's overseas activities, where he tripled the export business of the company, cut the cost of doing business overseas by a factor of ten, and added a number of ships to the company's inventory. Named President of U.S. Steel in 1911, Farrell continued to promote overseas development aggressively. He also solidified his foreign trade credentials as chair of the committees on foreign relations for American Iron and Steel Institute and the United States Chamber of Commerce.

Farrell never lost interest in maritime commerce. He founded the Isthmian Steamship Company in 1910 as a subsidiary of U.S. Steel for the purpose of taking advantage of the Panama Canal. Farrell was a globalization prophet and a pioneer of export markets who believed passionately in the importance of foreign trade. He practiced what he preached; during his time at the helm of U.S. Steel, he presided over a five-fold expansion, largely due to exports, turning it into America's first billion dollar industry. Farrell, Pennsylvania is named for him.

number of business councils and associations at the beginning of the twentieth century. Farrell's suggestions molded the early policy statements of the NFTC. This close connection between the Committee on Plan and Scope and the NFTC's policy positions through its first several decades was not surprising. Almost all committee participants were members of the American Manufacturers' Export Association, which espoused an expansionist outlook on foreign trade. And the committee itself was led by the first two chairmen of the NFTC: Farrell and Eugene Thomas. Farrell and Thomas were top executives at U.S. Steel, which increasingly derived a significant portion of its revenue from overseas. Other committee members were involved in finance, manufacturing, locomotives, and agriculture - all industries with growing overseas sales.[7]

Trade and the Wilson Administration

At the close of the first day's proceedings, and setting a one hundred year tradition delegates at the 1914 event dined at a black-tie banquet with the grandiose moniker World Trade Dinner. Secretary of State William Jennings Bryan delivered the keynoted address. Bryan outlined the Wilson Administration's plan to encourage American industry abroad. Like many of his advisers, Wilson viewed economic and strategic concerns as inseparable. The President's chief goal was to obtain equality of opportunity for American business in foreign markets.

However, on several occasions, Wilson had refused to support particular businesses trading overseas. He withdrew American participation in an international banking consortium in China that his predecessor William Howard Taft had encouraged; he refused to take protective custody of American-owned oil fields north of Veracruz, Mexico after ordering military occupation of this seaport, and he denied United Fruit's request that he recognize a new Central American government that the company had supported in a military coup.

Secretary Bryan acknowledged that while these specific decisions irked some businesses, what President Wilson and those gathered at the Hotel Raleigh shared was a belief in the need for expansionist policies that created liberal, open trading for American businesses. Bryan promised that the American government would lend its support to help resolve trade disputes through diplomatic and consular officials. Nevertheless, he warned the gathered delegates that the American government would not exert financial or political force in other sovereign nations. He ended by echoing Secretary of Commerce Redfield, emphasizing that private enterprise initiative and activity would have to drive American trade policy.[8]

President Wilson himself took great interest in foreign affairs - by necessity and also by virtue of personal interest, being a statesman at his core. This global interest extended to international trade. On the second afternoon of the convention, May

President Woodrow Wilson

28, the delegates adjourned until half past 3, where they reconvened in the East Room of the White House for a private reception with the President. Comically, Secretary of Commerce Redfield mistakenly waited alone for hours in the opposite end of the White House for the delegates to arrive, missing the very reception he had arranged. He sent an embarrassed note of apology to the Conventioneers later that same day.

Address of President Woodrow Wilson
to the National Foreign Trade Convention, May 28, 1914:

After recessing from the Hotel Raleigh, the delegates then proceeded to the White House where, in the East Room, they were received by the President, being individually introduced by Mr. Edward N. Hurley, Chairman of the Reception Committee. Addressing the delegates, the President said:

"I had hoped that Secretary Redfield would put into my ear what I should say to you, for I cannot claim to be an expert on the subjects you are discussing. I am sure he expressed the feeling which I would wish to express, which is the feeling of encouragement that is given by the gathering of a body like this for such a purpose. There is nothing in which I am more interested than the fullest development of the trade of this country and its righteous conquest of foreign markets.

"I think that you will realize from what Mr. Redfield has said to you that it is one of the things that we hold nearest to our heart that the government and you should co-operate in the most intimate manner in accomplishing our common object. One of your members just now said something in my ear about the merchant marine, and I am sure that I speak the conviction of all of you when I say that one of our chief needs is to have a merchant marine, because if we have to deliver our goods in other people's delivery wagons, their goods are delivered first and our goods are delivered incidentally on their routes. This is a matter I have had near my own heart for a great many years. It was only by authority of my parents that I was prevented from going to sea, and I only hope that it is not a universal regret that I did not.

"I hope this is only the first series of conferences of this sort with you gentleman, and I thank you for this opportunity."[9]

(President Wilson's remarks began a tradition of Presidential correspondence with the NFTC that would span a century. The NFTC Presidential Letter archive is displayed at NFTC headquarters in Washington, DC.)

Delegates had spent the morning of the convention's second day in sessions dedicated to the papers circulated prior to the convention. At each session, a chairman introduced the author of the paper and invited him to give a 10- to 15-minute synopsis. Following the synopsis, convention delegates were invited to comment, add their own insights, and ask questions of the author. Most comments lauded the paper or author, agreeing in broad strokes with the need for increased foreign trade. The papers covered a variety of topics from varying perspectives. Some presenters discussed the status of foreign trade in specific regions of the country. Others contained detailed, exhaustive information about the types and volumes of various export goods. A few authors investigated how American merchandise actually got to its intended destination, with a particular eye to questions of logistics and infrastructure. Other sessions explored modes of foreign trade, including ocean transportation, railroads, and vehicular export trade. Another set of speakers concentrated on particular problems with respect to American foreign trade policy, itself. Among these dilemmas: the ways the Sherman Antitrust Act might influence the quantity and operation of foreign trade, and how American firms might take advantage of new currency laws to increase their overseas trade. Finally, several experienced traders educated delegates on practical ways American businesses might begin to trade overseas, from market selection to appointing agents and distributors.

For the first time, one meeting had brought together all Americans engaged in foreign trade to hear comprehensive discussions about the problems and future of American trade. At the end of the convention, flush with success, delegates agreed to reconvene annually, which they did until the 1980s in one form or another.

Delegates also did something else incredibly important. In the very first resolution of the first National Foreign Trade Convention, in recognition that "…the Government and the industrial, commercial, transportation and financial interests should co-operate in an endeavor to extend our foreign trade," delegates unanimously called for the creation of an organization to "co-ordinate the foreign trade activities of the Nation." The newly minted group would examine issues facing American businesses engaged in foreign trade; make policy recommendations to the US government; cooperate with other national business associations; host future trade conventions; educate the public on the importance of international trade; and train private enterprise on its conduct. Its membership would be nationally representative, cutting across the economy to include all the diverse industries involved in foreign trade. It would be known as the National Foreign Trade Council.

Early Leaders and Members

The convention named James Farrell the first president of the newly-formed Council. This was probably a foregone conclusion. During the convention itself, Farrell had conducted business-driven strategic planning sessions about American foreign trade, and chaired the Committee on Plan and Scope, as well as the Finance Committee. All of this, plus his business leadership and foreign trade experience, made him the obvious choice to head an organization designed to coordinate and encourage policies to expand the foreign trade activities of the nation.[10]

The initial officers and members of the NFTC shared Farrell's views. The treasurer of the new group was Walter Clark, the vice president of New England Westinghouse, and the secretary was Robert Patchin, a former foreign correspondent for the *New York Herald* and later manager at W.R Grace. Manufacturers, such as Westinghouse, Lackawanna Steel, General Electric, and Anaconda Copper, dominated the membership. Financial institutions, like First National Bank, Security Trust and Savings Bank, National City Bank, and J. P Morgan also played an important role. Transportation and logistics concerns were also well-represented: Southern Railway, the Great Northern Railway, Baldwin Locomotives, American Locomotives, and the Robert Dollar Steamship Company. Members also included agriculture producers, like Hall-Baker Grain, International Harvester, and Portland Flouring Mills. There were members representing like-minded business groups, such as the Pan Asiatic Society and Galveston Cotton Exchange. Finally, several major chambers of commerce in export-focused cities, such as

Captain Robert Dollar

Robert Dollar (1844-1932) was born in Falkirk, Scotland. The title "Captain" was honorary as was his other title, the "Grand Old Man of the Pacific". Both were bestowed upon him after a lifetime in the shipping industry.

Dollar's early life was not easy. His mother died when he was nine years old, and he had to drop out of school to work, first in a machine shop, and then as an errand boy for a lumber company, to help support his family. His father remarried and moved the family to Canada where Dollar began working in a lumber camp at age 14 as a cook's helper. He learned French and, at the age of 17, became a logger. At the age of thirty he married, had four children and invested in a lumber venture that failed. Heavily in debt ($2,500), he was determined to pay off his share, which he did in full. Dollar learned from his mistakes and carefully bought other lumber camps that were successful, not only in Michigan but in Northern California.

Frustrated by the lack of reliable shipping, in 1895 he acquired his first vessel to move lumber rapidly from the Pacific Northwest to markets down the coast. This led within a decade to the Dollar Steamship Company, whose ships plied the Pacific and were a common sight during the interwar years from Canada and California to Canton, Shanghai, and Tokyo. In 1923, he pioneered a successful round-the-world passenger service that came to be known as the American President Lines (today known as APL). At the time of his death, the net worth of this immigrant participant in the American Dream was $40 million ($683 million in 2014 dollars). He was so prominent a citizen that he became known as 'The Dean of American Shipping' and even appeared on the cover of Time magazine.

After his death, with the support of his family, the NFTC created the Captain Robert Dollar Memorial Award. In 1938, the first of these awards was presented to U.S. Secretary of State Cordell Hull for his work opening new markets to American trade. The awards continued to be given until the mid-1980s, then were revived in 2002 as the World Trade Award.

Boston, Pittsburgh, Norfolk, and Mobile were founding members of the Council. (See Appendix of Founding Members of the NFTC).

First Policy Recommendations

Upon its formation, the NFTC issued recommendations for America trade policy. These reflected a liberal, expansionist worldview, and, on the whole, the NFTC has hewed consistently to these policy goals during its entire 100 year existence. It first adopted a resolution favoring the reorganization of the Bureau of Foreign and Domestic Commerce. This governmental body had been formed in the early 20th century to assist American firms in foreign trade matters. However, the bureau had few personnel and existed in a bureaucratic limbo, residing in both the Departments of State and Commerce. This led to complications and inefficiencies; many delegates at the convention complained about a lack of response and general ineffectiveness of the Bureau. In order to help remedy the situation, the NFTC supported a resolution made by Redfield, strengthening the bureau's numbers of staff and budget, and placing it solely in the Department of Commerce. This was the precursor agency to today's Foreign and Commercial Service (FCS).

In a similar vein, the Council also pledged support for a larger and more robust consular service. The State Department employed only a handful of individuals in American embassies to assist American firms in their overseas commercial activities. It helped firms make connections with foreign companies and helped to resolve trade disputes. The Council suggested increasing their ranks, and members believed the State Department could encourage more qualified applicants by offering better salaries.

Likewise, the Council also called for the State Department to take a more active role in negotiating commercial treaties. The State Department could make deals to open up closed markets to American companies. The NFTC saw these treaties as a way to bypass some of the onerous protectionist schemes imposed on American goods by foreign governments.

Believing in the importance of government assistance in trade expansion, the NFTC supported government-led efforts to strengthen American foreign trade. For example, it favored strengthening America's merchant marine. At the first convention, several speakers noted with approbation that most American exports no longer travelled on American-built ships. Among these speakers included Captain Robert Dollar, head of Dollar Steamship; and President Wilson even mentioned the issue in his informal East Room remarks to the delegates. Shipping magnates saw the loss of shipping market share as deleterious to American business, as it unnecessarily increased prices. Dollar, as one of the first and most active members of the Council, supported a governmental program to support the building and operation of American-built, privately owned ships.

Members of the Council believed that the lack of a comprehensive trade policy reflected a failure to appreciate the connection between national prosperity and foreign trade. They called for a national program of education to make this link clearer. These educational efforts would broaden over time to encompass a wide range of activities demonstrating the importance of trade to American lives.

Finally, the NFTC resolved to support legislation that would allow American firms to cooperate overseas. The Council praised the Federal Reserve Act of 1913, which had allowed American banks to operate more easily and cooperatively overseas. American antitrust laws, like the Sherman Act, seemingly prevented American businesses from working together or sharing information when operating overseas. The Council feared the Sherman Antitrust Act could be used to prosecute corporate cooperation in overseas trade, the threat of which would frighten smaller manufacturers from entering foreign trade. Therefore, one of the Council's first set of formal policy recommendations proposed ways that firms could increase overseas cooperation, yet remain confident that they would not run afoul of the act.[11]

The NFTC issued these policy proposals at its first regular board meeting which was held in September 1914 in New York City. There the Council adopted an organizational structure similar to that of the convention. Much of the early work of the Council took place in committees that reflected the visions and priorities of the organization for the coming year. Early committees included education, merchant marine, tariffs, treaties, and, with an eye toward cooperative efforts with other trade associations and to reinforce the connections of Farrell and other Council members, collaboration with the United States Chamber of Commerce. Reflecting the need for continued cooperation of American business in expansionist endeavors, the Council used its authority to call another national foreign trade convention for January 1915.[12]

Opportunities in Latin America

In late 1914, the Council issued its first regional report. In it, the authors highlighted the importance of Latin American coffee and rubber to the United States, but they also stressed the challenges and problems in the Latin American market. America lacked capital investments and financial instruments in Latin America necessary to promote trade or the production of raw materials. Because of existing financial laws preventing American banks from operating extensively overseas, U.S. firms operating in Latin America were almost wholly reliant on London banks for financing. With European lending squeezed during the war years, the NFTC suggested steps to insure the expansion of American trade in Latin America. American banks needed to be able to open branches in South America; American ships needed to move exports and imports; and business and the government needed to make more investments in Latin America. The report also warned that the trade vacuum created by the war would not automatically deliver South American trade to the United States. Germany and England had both made significant investments in railways and industrial, agricultural, and mining enterprises. Increasing infrastructure investment in Latin America would provide lasting economic security to the United States through access to raw materials and markets and prepare for the post-war trade landscape.[13]

The Great War - Initial Impacts

Beyond its longer-term goals, the Council faced immediate work with the war raging in Europe. American businesses experienced steep declines in exports during the first few months of the conflict, but they realized they had an extraordinary opportunity. With European goods and capital diverted to the trenches, American traders could fill the void, especially to emerging markets like Latin America. To respond to these circumstances, the Council held an emergency meeting in August 1914. It first sought to protect Americans at sea and abroad. The Council issued a "vigorous call" to the federal government to enact ship registry legislation and establish a robust system of war risk insurance. Foreshadowing later efforts, the Council called for warring nations to do away with economic embargoes. European nations had issued these to exert economic pressure on their enemies, but the NFTC saw these kinds of trade sanctions as damaging to everyone, including those imposing them.

As the war in Europe deepened, members of the Council were proven correct in their assumption that the conflict could help Americans trading abroad. American exporters rushed to make up the difference of declining European production, and, as a result of their successes, America amassed significant sums of gold bullion during the course of the war, and as a consequence became the world's greatest capital-exporting nation. Acquisition of gold reserves turned America from the largest global debtor to the world's preeminent creditor nation within a decade. This transition fueled a massive expansion of the American economy. Capital inflows allowed American businesses to make significant investments abroad, and allowed American bankers to vastly expand their overseas lending, particularly to Latin America.

As a result, some members of the NFTC believed the war vividly demonstrated to all Americans the connection between national prosperity and the welfare of foreign trade. Initially, citizens experienced wartime shortages of various goods and necessities, then witnessed the marvelous capacity of American business traders and investors to fill these market gaps both domestically and in far-flung international markets, resulting in unprecedented expansion of manufacturing, the establishment of new distribution networks, and a surge in employment.[14]

Yet, despite these positive developments, the leadership of NFTC now worried that the American government and private business were not fully in position to exploit them, echoing the concerns which led to the first foreign trade convention. At the second meeting of the Council's board of directors, James Farrell underscored his belief that America's progress from debtor to creditor was merely serendipitous. He believed it had nothing to do with improvements in the nation's commercial conditions, but rather that the increase in US exports was due solely to the European conflict, since American trade to other regions had, in fact, *decreased*. Farrell further said that despite appearances, the nation was ill-equipped to trade in foreign markets. The government did not coordinate American foreign policy with private investment aims in foreign countries, "which would fortify their advantage after the war." Coordination of policy with direct investment in regions such as Latin America could secure a long term preference for American trading partners and provide a path forward for American foreign trade.[15] This marked the start of the Council's still ongoing efforts to coordinate US foreign policy with the investment aims of the private sector, with varying degrees of success over the years.

The Great War - The Role of Foreign Trade

The NFTC believed that foreign trade would play as pivotal a role in winning the Great War as it did in creating national prosperity. When the nation transitioned from spectator to participant in the conflict, the Council increasingly focused on ways to aid the war effort. Meeting in 1918 at the Fifth National Foreign Trade Convention, the Council resolved that the objective of the convention and the Council was "to consider the part of foreign trade in winning the war." Even though American firms would naturally be planning for the expansion of American exports once the war concluded, this discussion needed to be subordinated to measures that "will impose new and heavy penalties on our (wartime) adversaries." To that end, industry trade groups submitted reports outlining the ways various sectors of the American economy could quicken victory.[16]

Foreign trade supported national credit and provided the raw materials needed to continue military and naval efforts. In turn, war policies strengthened American trade. As European sources of trade declined, the nations of Latin America and Asia grew dependent upon American merchandise to sustain their rising exports of raw materials. The United States correspondingly relied upon these nations for essential war materials and food. By the time the war neared its end, both war and economic policy dictated that American should continue this reciprocal arrangement.

In this way, the war years also afforded the Council an opportunity to advance other parts of its agenda. The decline in European trade to Latin America, for example, had provided an opportunity for American investors and financiers to fill the vacuum. Latin America's status as an emerging market had long been of interest to Americans trading abroad, and this continued during the war years. The NFTC investigated the status of U.S.-Latin American trade for the Commerce Department, to ensure that the short term foothold in these markets would be leveraged for the long term advantage of American exporters.

The US Merchant Marine

The Council also used the war years to advocate its position on the importance of the American merchant marine. The 1918 convention declaration noted "the imperative need of the hour is the presence in the North Atlantic of as great tonnage as can be handled," without weakening supply lines to non-European nations. The war had created a unique set of problems for American shipping. Eastern ports were extremely crowded, and had little spare capacity. Southern ports had more space, but lacked improved waterways and modern facilities. The First World War had also exacerbated shortages in shipping capacity, as the government took control of privately owned ships in support of the war effort.

Beginning at this time and for years afterward, the Council pressed the government for a systematic merchant marine policy for the return of commandeered ships to private ownership, and to mitigate against future government takeovers. The NFTC fashioned a merchant marine policy that called for private ownership of all merchant marine vessels; the creation of a permanent shipping board made up of experienced shippers; and called for policies resulting in "private investments in American shipping to be made safe and attractive." Members of the Council would eventually get their wish with the passage of the Merchant Marine Act in 1928, which placed American shipping on equal footing with other shipping nations and financed the construction of privately owned ships. The legislative battle was a long one. It took years to pass the bill, and the Council was never really satisfied with its implementation.[17]

In later years, the Council would look back at these early days as some of the most important in American trade. American exports exploded into world markets, capturing market share it would hold for decades. American businesses now gathered annually to educate one another on issues and opportunities abroad. American traders now spoke with a unified voice to guide US trade policy in a way never done before. And at the center of it all stood the National Foreign Trade Council.

Chapter Endnotes

1 "To Encourage Oversea Trade," *New York Times*, May 11, 1914.

2 Ibid; "Official Report of the National Foreign Trade Convention," National Foreign Trade Convention, 1914.

3 "Official Report of the National Foreign Trade Convention," 203.

4 "Official Report of the National Foreign Trade Convention."

5 Ibid.

6 Ibid.

7 "Bryan Draws Line at Force in Trade," *New York Times*, May 28, 1914.

8 Ibid.

9 "Official Report of the National Foreign Trade Convention."

10 "J.A. Farrell Dies; U.S. Steel Ex-Head," *New York Times* March 29, 1943.

11 "How Smaller Manufacturers May Succeed as Exporters," *Wall Street Journal*, January 22, 1915.

12 "For Overseas Trade," *New York Times*, September 17, 1914.

13 "Reports on trade of South America," *New York Times*, September 8, 1914.

14 Chairmen's Report in "Second Annual Meeting, The National Foreign Trade Council", September 1915, National Foreign Trade Council Records, Box 24, Folder 11.

15 Ibid.

16 "Final Declaration of the Fifth National Foreign Trade Convention, April 18-20, 1918", April 1918, National Foreign Trade Council Records, Box 78, Folder 12.

17 "Board of Ship Men to Modernize Laws," *New York Times*, October 27, 1915; "Final Declaration of the Sixteenth National Foreign Trade Convention", April 1929, National Foreign Trade Council Records, Box 78, Folder 21; "Final Declaration of the Twenty-First National Foreign Trade Convention", November 1934, National Foreign Trade Council Records, Box 78, Folder 26; "Official Report of the National Foreign Trade Convention"; "Final Declaration of the Sixth National Foreign Trade Convention," National Foreign Trade Council Records, Box 78, Folder 13.

CHAPTER TWO

Growing in Size and Influence

DOWNTOWN BUSINESS MEN ORGANIZE TO FOSTER FOREIGN TRADE
New York Times (1857-1922); Sep 27, 1914;
ProQuest Historical Newspapers The New York Times (1851 - 2007)
pg. SM2

DOWNTOWN BUSINESS MEN ORGANIZE TO FOSTER FOREIGN TRADE

India House, Hanover Square, New York

Home to the National Foreign Trade Council, 1914-1948

India House

The NFTC made these early policy decisions out of its offices at India House[1] in New York City. Located on Hanover Square just blocks from Wall Street, India House is walking distance from both the offices of international financiers and the East River docks, providing a convenient meeting place for all Americans engaged in overseas trade, the vast majority of which passed through the Port of New York during this era. Consequently, the early histories of the NFTC and India House were closely intertwined.

With the founding of the NFTC to promote expansion of all America's foreign trade activities, its founders sought to establish "a much needed headquarters for the various interests that have to do with foreign commerce" in the United States. This group of individuals, again led by James Farrell, visualized a central meeting place that would "bring together men concerned with foreign trade, many of whom, now doing business within a couple of blocks of one another, have never met." Other trade associations had meeting places, and it was time for America's foreign traders and investors to have a gathering place to call their own.[2]

Several of the founders of the NFTC—James Farrell, Willard Straight, Robert Patchin, and the presidents of the Lackawanna Steel Company, Dollar

Steamship Company, W.R. Grace Shipping, Chase National Bank, and United States Rubber joined together to lease an old Renaissance palazzo style building "on the boundary line between the financial section and the spicy district extending to the East River, devoted since the early days to the importing and trading interests." Much earlier it was home to the Hanover Bank, then later to the New York Cotton Exchange and W.R. Grace Shipping. The interior was gutted and renovated, and the exterior painstakingly restored. Early leaders of the NFTC, notably James Farrell, A.W. Drake, Willard Straight and his wife Dorothy Whitney, filled the inside of the building with paintings and engravings of famous American merchant ships, highlighting their expansionist mindset and hearkening back to the romantic heyday of the clipper ships. These artifacts gave India House and the NFTC both prestige and cultural cachet. According to the *New York Times*, not even the Metropolitan Museum of Art had as fine a collection of model ships as India House, and as the logical home of models of Columbus' ships, the Council continued Columbus' legacy of "foreign [trade]…with an extra-large cargo of courage and imagination."[3]

The name India House was chosen to evoke distant overseas markets (never mind that none of the founders actually traded there) and to pay homage to the Dutch East India Company, the original colonizers of Manhattan. Against the myriad economic and legislative changes during the early twentieth century, India House and its tenant/sister the NFTC would play a major role in fostering cooperation and information-sharing among U.S. trading interests, all with the aim of increasing American foreign trade.

The earliest NFTC logo, circa 1915.

The emphasis on India House and New York City reflect the prominence of each in early 20th Century international trade.

As Farrell and his colleagues had envisioned, India House served as a convenient meetinghouse for U.S. businessmen doing commerce all over the world. Over the years, it became the headquarters to a number of specialized business and trade associations with interest overseas, helping solidify ties to the NFTC. As one example, as U.S. business interests in Latin

America increased in the first third of the twentieth century, in 1930 the NFTC established the Committee on Inter-American Cooperation (CIAC). This group coordinated the activities "of the numerous organizations existent in the United States with programs aimed at better understanding with the countries between the Rio Grande and the Straits of Magellan." The headquarters of the CIAC was in India House, allowing easy coordination with the NFTC.

The Annual Meeting of the Board

India House also served as the location for many annual meetings of the governing board of the NFTC. Usually held in the fall, the annual meeting of the governing members and the board of directors was the one of the biggest and most important events of the year for the Council. Only the conventions drew a larger audience. The NFTC used these sessions to discuss its activities and priorities for the coming year, including Council positions, publications, advocacy efforts, committee work, and budgetary matters.

Reflecting the informal, networking qualities of the Council, one of the most exciting, and well-attended parts of the annual board meeting was a lavish dinner. The 1940 dinner, which drew 75 to 100 people to the opulent Marine Room of India House, was representative. Farrell believed these dinners provided a unique opportunity to gather America's most important foreign traders in one room. Farrell sat at the head of the table with the room's fireplace behind him, Eugene Thomas — the U.S. Steel executive and Council officer — on one side, and Farrell's son, founder of the eponymously named shipping company, on the other. During the dinner, Farrell, other members of the Council, and selected businessmen spoke candidly and gave remarks of "considerable interest" about the condition of foreign trade in the United States. American traders and investors could acquire vital knowledge about overseas trade from these dinners.

The Council spared no expense for these dinners. Organizers of the 1940 dinner settled on a seven-course meal, consisting of diamondback terrapin soup, madeira, and hot butter crescents; celery and olives; grilled fillets of sole, fine herbs, cucumber, sauté doria, and corn sticks; filet mignon, excelsior buttered new peas, potatoes macaire; hearts of romaine, melon and grapefruit, and orange dressing; spumoni ice cream, anis madeleines; and coffee. Eugene Thomas, now president of the NFTC, said he selected this menu to recreate a Jefferson-Jackson dinner he had attended earlier in the year in the Midwest.[4]

Among the many decisions made by the Council's board at the annual fall meeting was selecting the location for the annual convention. There was significant competition for the annual foreign trade convention, as thousands of delegates and their families attended these events. Representatives from local Chambers of Commerce, mayors, and other local government officials lobbied the NFTC and highlighted their hotel accommodations, the number of potential delegates, and the investment opportunities in their city.

The National Foreign Trade Convention

During the first several decades of its existence, the annual conventions were the most important activity of the Council. Early on, they resembled the information-gathering-and-distributing quality of the first meeting. After a few years, the pre-circulation of papers and formal comments. Delegates no longer obtained copies of speeches in advance—they now had to wait until the conclusion of the convention to receive papers along with the official proceedings.[5]

Delegates paid what was considered a high $10 registration fee to attend the early conventions. The fee defrayed some of the expenses of the convention. The Council sent out invitations to potential attendees, rather than relying upon a permanent membership. Convention organizers intended that the registration fee, invitations, and lack of frivolous entertainment would have the effect of restricting the gathering to the most serious and prestigious American traders.[6]

The annual convention developed certain patterns and habits in these early decades. Convention delegates wore "distinctive badges." Usually red, they provided the delegate's name and the firm represented. The convention typically opened on a Monday, with the First General Session set for 9:30 a.m. After the chairman called the session to order, he customarily gave a speech on the current condition of foreign trade. Farrell occupied this privileged speaking position until his death in 1943.

Following Farrell's speech, a prominent individual, such as a Cabinet member or under-secretary, greeted the delegates on behalf of the president of the United States. This highlighted the close relationship with the Council and the federal government during the first several decades of its existence. Continuing after the Wilson Administration, most presidents and their administrations shared Wilson's liberal, expansionist view of foreign trade. This speaker would highlight this shared view and discussed how the government planned to work with Americans engaged in foreign trade to expand overseas opportunities.

Eugene Thomas, who had become president of the NFTC in the 1932, also acquired a regular speaking slot. In his speech, he usually discussed the activities of the NFTC for the upcoming year.[7]

NFTC President Eugene Thomas, 1932-50; and Chairman 1943-45.

PROGRAM

25th

NATIONAL
FOREIGN TRADE
CONVENTION

NEW YORK
Hotel Commodore
OCT. 31, NOV. 1 & 2
1938

Growth of the National Foreign Trade Convention

The Convention Committee, comprised of more than 100 members, worked year-round on the logistics of the convention to ensure its success. Chairmen and vice chairmen headed efforts to make local arrangements, suggest speakers, and plan the theme and scope of the convention. Along these lines, the Council also had regional convention committees. These local bodies drummed up support for the convention in particular states or regions. Members reached out to local firms, wrote opinion pieces for newspapers, and appeared on the radio to promote the activities of the NFTC and the annual convention. The Council's executive officers kept in touch with these local committees, using them to estimate the number of attendees at the convention and to encourage prominent traders to serve as speakers.[8]

As the conventions expanded, the early strictures against entertainment were dropped, and parallel social gatherings evolved. The Council now actively encouraged these activities, seeing them as vital in attracting a large attendance by encouraging delegates to bring their families along. A Women's Reception Committee was established specifically to plan activities for the wives and families of conventioneers. Social activities for the delegates and their families grew more elaborate, especially when the site of the convention was also a popular tourist destination. For example, at the 1930 convention in Los Angeles, the Women's Reception Committee organized a luncheon for the wives of delegates at Paramount Studios, where "they would have the opportunity to see Movietone pictures in the making" or to visit the San Gabriel mission. At the same convention, "visiting delegates and ladies were the guests of the L.A. steamship company on an all-day ocean outing" including a visit to the Catalina Islands.[9]

The Council used both the content and location of the convention as a marketing tool to promote the meeting. When advertising the convention, the Council usually sent out a proposed program of events designed to pique the interest of

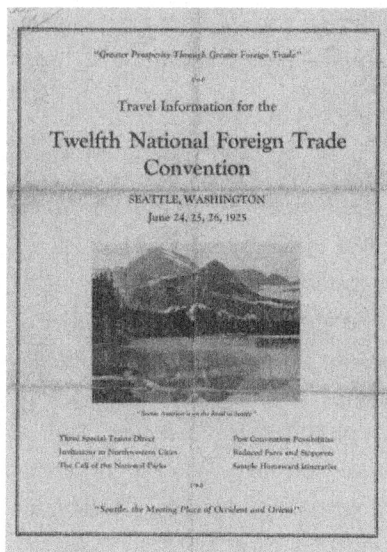

"Greater Prosperity Through Greater Foreign Trade"

Travel Information for the

Twelfth National Foreign Trade Convention

SEATTLE, WASHINGTON
June 24, 25, 26, 1925

"Scenic America is on the Road to Seattle"

Three Special Trains Direct
Invitations to Northwestern Cities
The Call of the National Parks

Post Convention Possibilities
Reduced Fares and Stopovers
Sample Homeward Itineraries

"Seattle, the Meeting Place of Occident and Orient!"

Americans engaged in foreign trade. It would also include a list of "representatives at the convention of the United States government and of independent offices and establishments." The potential to meet and discuss issues of trade with leaders and officers of various cabinet departments, commissions, and financial institutions provided a unique opportunity for Americans involved in overseas trade.

Promotional materials also emphasized the unique features of the convention sites. For example, the brochure cover for the June 1925 meeting in Seattle showed the Cascade Mountains and remarked that Seattle was "the Meeting Place of Occident and Orient." The brochure promised direct trains to the convention from the East Coast (the "foreign trade specials"), special activities in the cities of the Northwest, and the opportunity to heed the "call of the national parks." The Seattle convention promised "travel through the greatest scenic marvels of the American continent." Delegates could use the convention for their summer travel, as it was occurring "just as the vacation season opens." As they returned home, attendees could stop at Glacier National Park for a tour "including a day trip by bus and lake launch over the park" with "an entertainment by Blackfeet Indians."[10] The Council also offered post-Convention possibilities, such as a trade mission to the Far East on a specially arranged Admiral-Orient ship, where delegates could discuss the convention and connect with delegates from India, China, Japan, the Philippines, and the Dutch East Indies.[11]

Highlighting the personal nature of the conventions, amusing and awkward encounters often occurred. Paul Leake, collector of customs for the Port of San Francisco, attended the 1940 convention in San Francisco incognito. After attending the importers' group session, the executive secretary of the National Council of Importers asked Leake why he did not formally participate in the session. Leake said he was afraid he would be the subject of indignation for all the customs collecting he did. The son of William Jennings Bryan attended the same convention. In the hallway, between sessions, "a 92 year old man stopped him and said he had voted for his father three times, and come November, he was going to do it again." Since the elder Bryan had died nearly a decade earlier, this would have proved difficult.[12]

As the size and scope of the convention increased, various trade groups and association began to latch their own annual meetings or gatherings onto it. The Bankers Association for Foreign Trade usually sponsored a session and held a luncheon centering on the problems of banking and American foreign trade. Other groups taking advantage of the drawing power of the National Foreign Trade Convention included the Export Advertising Association, the Export Managers Club of New York, the Foreign Credit Interchange Bureau of the National Association of Credit Men, the National Council of American Importers, and many others.[13]

To fulfill one of its objectives to serve as a clearinghouse for information about foreign trade, the Council provided trade advisers at the convention. The Council connected government officials and private businessmen with delegates wishing to acquire knowledge about the overseas trade. This trade adviser service became one of the most popular parts of the convention, particularly during the Great Depression. As it became more popular, the Council expanded this program into the Trade Promotion Service. At a convention dinner, organizers promised that "delegates...will be seated" with the trade adviser of their choice. There were no set speeches or discussions. Advisers, wearing red badges, sat at each table to dispense "disinterested trade advice...about any foreign trade problem" to their dining partners. [14]

The World Trade Dinner

The highlight of every foreign trade convention was the World Trade Dinner. This black-tie banquet brought together all of the thousands of delegates to hear speeches, discuss various trade matters, connect with the leading foreign traders of the day, and praise American foreign trade efforts. The dinner usually sold out weeks in advance and typically attracted the most media attention. Radio networks broadcast the keynote addresses from these dinners, and writers from papers around the nation attended en masse. In 1938, for example, NBC transmitted speeches by Secretary of State Cordell Hull and the ambassador of Brazil.[15]

The World Trade Dinners often highlighted the location of the convention, usually in some dramatic fashion. At the 1930 convention, held in Los Angeles, delegates watched a Movietone film shot the previous month in Japan. Most of the convention had focused on the increasing business opportunities for Americans in the Far East, and this film underscored this emphasis. The Japanese government had sent it as a token of Japanese-American friendship. The movie highlighted Japanese landscapes, cities, and potential business possibilities for American firms.[16]

Captain Robert Dollar Memorial Award

The World Trade Dinner also became the occasion for the annual presentation of the Captain Robert Dollar Memorial Award. The award initially recognized the individual who had contributed most to the expansion of American foreign trade in the previous year; it later praised those who had made lifelong contributions to trade. The Dollar Family of San Francisco established the award in 1937 in memory of Captain Robert Dollar, a pioneer in American shipping and founding member of the NFTC (see inset page 12). [17]

In 1938, the Award Committee bestowed the first award on Secretary of State Cordell Hull, in recognition of his years of efforts in expanding U.S. trade through Reciprocal Trade Agreements, which allowed the president to negotiate reduced tariffs with trading partners in return for reciprocal reductions in U.S. tariffs. Other early award winners included James Farrell, first chairman of the NFTC, president of India House, and president of US Steel; Eric Johnston, president of the United States Chamber of Commerce; Thomas Watson, president of IBM and the International Chamber of Commerce; Eugene Thomas, president of the NFTC and vice president of US Steel; Sumner Welles, Undersecretary of State; Juan Trippe, president of PanAm; and many other notable foreign trade luminaries. (See Appendix D for full list of *Captain Robert Dollar Memorial Award* and *World Trade Award* winners.)

1940 Dollar Award Citation of Thomas Watson, Chairman and CEO of IBM

Dollar Award winners always addressed the delegates, a speech closely watched by Americans engaged in foreign trade. In 1940, Watson received the award for his contributions to foreign trade, particularly as president of the International Chamber of Commerce. His speech, occurring in the first years of the Second World War, focused on the ways the conflict had affected the normal flow of goods, and how he believed that that flow would resume at the conclusion of the war based upon Cordell Hull's Reciprocal Trade Agreements. He also urged Americans to cooperate with South American countries in developing their natural resources. He concluded by encouraging delegates to visualize a new era of what he called 'internationalization' of commerce, and by citing the golden rule as a good guiding principle of foreign trade.[18]

Dollar Memorial Award Winners, 1956-1966. At bottom right is NFTC President William Swingle (1950-62).

The Captain Robert Dollar Memorial Award was presented annually well into the 1980's. It was revived in 2002 by the NFTC Board of Directors as the World Trade Award, "in the spirit of the Captain Robert Dollar Memorial Award." It is still presented annually in recognition of lifetime achievement in advancing open, rules-based global trade and investment.

The Conference Declaration

At the end of every conference, convention delegates issued a declaration of their positions on important foreign trade issues. Delegates chose a Convention Committee on the first day of the convention, usually consisting of Council members and other significant traders, to decide which issues would be included in the declaration. The convention declaration generally presented the policies the delegates wanted the government to adopt and/or the priorities for the NFTC in the coming year. The declarations differed notably during times of crisis, such as wars and economic downturns.

The 1930 convention declaration provides an illustrative example, with the Great Depression as its backdrop. It eschewed a litany of specific policy proposals for a tone of resigned encouragement. The precipitous decline in world trade was because "the world has become one great market, every part of which is quickly sensitive to conditions in other parts." The convention hoped renewal of foreign investments in the United States would improve economic conditions by increasing the supply of dollars in the marketplace and by lowering interest rates. The declaration encouraged convention delegates to cooperate with the government to restore public confidence and stabilize industrial conditions. The United States should not adopt protectionist trade policies; policies like these show "the failure to understand international trade," a thinly veiled reference to Smoot-Hawley legislation then before Congress. Summing up the beliefs of the NFTC, the Council promised to work for policies of "justice and fair play between nations." These could only be maintained through the development of the bonds of commercial friendship and mutual understanding.[19]

An Unbiased, Expert Approach to Trade

The principles of rules and fairness best describe the Council's policy of providing "non-political and non-partisan consideration of problems arising in foreign trade." While most early founders and members of the NFTC shared a liberal, expansionist vision of trade with Democrats like President Wilson, the Council eschewed supporting political parties. It invited both Democrats and Republicans to speak to its meetings and conventions, and intentionally avoided modern forms of political lobbying. While Council members occasionally testified before Congress or advocated their views in convention declarations, the Council saw these activities as informational in character. Members of the Council believed that its foreign-trade expertise gave it a unique ability to serve as an unbiased source of advice to policy makers and the ability to educate all Americans in the important connection between national prosperity and foreign trade.

To project its expertise and dispense advice, the Council created several committees to carry out long-term projects. These early committees addressed finances, publicity, membership, merchant marine issues, reciprocal trade agreements, and several other issues. Special committees also formed around short-term issues, like war losses. The Council also had several cooperating organizations. These groups operated under the auspices or along with the Council in specific areas. Cooperating organizations included regionally specific organizations, such as the Committee on Inter-American Cooperation (CIAC), the American-Chinese Trade Council, as well as the Joint Committee for Foreign Trade Action.[20]

The Council and its committees had an active first few decades. On some occasions, the Council played important roles in convincing foreign nations or firms to release the frozen funds of member companies. By the early 1930s, the NFTC had helped to release $100 million of blocked funds held by foreign governments, helping to resolve the claims of more than 1,200 creditors. Efforts to release frozen balances often worked in tandem with attempts to ease exchange restrictions. Long believing in open access to foreign markets, the NFTC pushed for foreign nations to eliminate policies that discriminated against American firms, such as currency blocs, exchange controls, barter, and other artificial restrictions. In one instance, the Council worked in conjunction with the CIAC and the Committee on Exchange Restrictions to negotiate exchange agreements with Brazil and Argentina. In 1937, these negotiations resulted in the freeing of $38 million in frozen American funds and increased trade between the countries.

The Council's advocacy on legal matters aligned with its efforts to adjudicate and resolve trade problems. In one case, Cambria Steel wanted to lead the formation of an export company to be called American Steel Export, with the goal of uniting the efforts of several steel companies to market and trade their goods overseas. However, the president of Cambria Steel, W.H. Donner, believed the Sherman antitrust law would prevent the formation of this export company. He appealed to the Council for assistance. In response, the NFTC prepared a detailed report about the situation and drafted an amendment for Congressional consideration that would allow American Steel Export to move forward.[21]

The Council also worked to resolve trade problems between foreign nations and American companies. Early in the summer of 1919, the NFTC received a letter from the senior British trade commissioner in Australia. The letter complained that American exporters misused the term FOB (Freight On Board) when shipping goods to Australia. The commissioner complained that American companies interpreted FOB differently than Australian firms and in a manner that was at variance with prevailing international procedures. The executive board of the Council took up the issue, issuing a letter to American exporters urging them to adopt standard shipping practices. An accepted, regular set of practices would help prevent trade disputes. This fracas fit in with one of the Council's larger projects during its early years of existence: pressing American exporters and shipping companies to standardize shipping quotations. Largely successful in this endeavor, the Council held meetings with various shipping parties, and it published a book with standard terms and quotations, which was one of its most successful and widely requested publications.[22] It is one of the precursors of today's Incoterms.

On occasion, the NFTC chose not to get involved in particular trade disputes. Sometimes, members wanted the organization to remain impartial and nonpartisan. Other times, it lacked the staff or resources to adjudicate the specific problem. For example, two American shipping companies complained to the NFTC because they had had shipments rejected at the port of London. Port authorities denied entry to the American goods on grounds of "faulty or insufficient delivery." The secretary of the Council investigated both cases and realized that the issue was beyond the scope and function of the Council. He was able to transfer the issue to the United States Chamber of Commerce, which was "better equipped for the situation."[23]

**NFTC educational materials of the 1930's
spoke to the average American.**

Education Efforts

A substantial portion of the Council's actions consisted of educating on foreign trade issues and sharing information with member companies. The NFTC published hundreds of reports, pamphlets, and bulletins annually with intelligence about issues such as tariff policies, foreign markets, and merchandising, as well as on the Council's actions. The mailing operation was sophisticated, with Council members sent reports relevant to their specific interests. So, while everyone received a copy of Chairman Farrell's World Trade Dinner speech, only interested parties received bulletins on agricultural commodities in Latin America. The NFTC also sent material to local Chambers of Commerce, university and college libraries, newspapers, and other interested parties. A significant portion of the Council's budget went into publishing these various documents. In 1938, Council publications addressed the exchange situation in Brazil and Turkey, the farmer's stake in foreign markets, the most-favored-nation agreement with Greece, economic conditions in Ireland, trading with the Communist nations of Eastern Europe, and many others.

One of the most popular of these early publications was a pamphlet entitled "Starting to Export." This made sense, as American businesses increasingly sought information about how to begin trading overseas. The NFTC had members and staff who had long traded overseas. The NFTC prepared a pamphlet with the elementary steps to enter the export trade, the sources of information businesses should consult, and the most important policies they should pay attention.[24]

President Franklin D. Roosevelt signing the Reciprocal Trade Agreements Act of 1934, with Secretary of State Cordell Hull and others as witnesses.

Early Advocacy Successes

Through its advocacy efforts, the Council worked to make foreign trade more equitable. During these early years, this meant supporting Reciprocal Trade Agreements. Envisaged by Secretary of State Cordell Hull as a way to replace a patchwork system of trade rules and to repair the Depression-era economy, the Reciprocal Trade Agreements Act of 1934 gave the president the power to negotiate bilateral, reciprocal trade agreements with other countries. This policy continued the liberal, expansionist policy of involving the government in opening up markets for American companies. These acts also gave Congress an incentive to lower tariffs because it tied tariff reductions to reciprocal reductions in other countries. These more liberal trade policies appealed to the Council's desire for a fairer system, which it believed would eliminate many of the trade problems occurring in international finance, like trade barriers, quotas, restrictions, and discriminatory policies.

The NFTC especially favored the Reciprocal Trade Agreements because they replaced the Smoot-Hawley Tariff Act with a system of international trade based on cooperation. In the Council's opinion, the Smoot-Hawley act was protectionist legislation prevented American businesses from obtain a large share of the world market. For the Council, the Reciprocal Trade Agreements Act was so successful because moving trade policy from Congress to the executive branch was the quickest way to advance trade expansion and domestic economic growth. The Council shared this view with the National Automobile Chamber of Commerce, the American Manufacturers' Export Association, and the Foreign Commerce Club of New York.

The Council was lucky that its policy proposals had support from internationalist voices within the government. Located in the State Department and the Federal Reserve, men like Secretary Hull had free reign over American trade policy. Franklin Delano Roosevelt's trade adviser, by ironic contrast, was the protectionist George Peek. Hull, like the Council, believed a peaceful world order depended on an open international economy and tighter commercial ties. He called for the president to have authority over bilateral trade agreements and tariff policy, a radical departure from previous trade policy. While wrapped in notions of domestic prosperity, what bound Hull and the NFTC was a core belief in an open, rules-based world trading system.[25]

During this era, the Council also actively supported a comprehensive shipping bill, a robust consular service, and favorable taxation policies. Early on, it asked the Department of Commerce to establish an aviation division to promote air travel and pushed for low-cost mail and telegraph services. It commended the establishment of the Export-Import Bank in 1934 and contemporaneous attempts to balance the federal budget because these activities provided financing for American traders and ensured a strong dollar, favorable to exporters.

Another of the Councils' first major victories was convincing the federal government to stop double taxation. American overseas traders had long complained about the practice of being taxed in the country they conducted business, and then taxed again in the United States. The NFTC made this one of its first causes and succeeded in repealing the policy.

By uniting the wide community of export traders under one umbrella and by speaking with one voice, the NFTC was notably successful in its early advocacy efforts.

Budget Woes and Member Dues

In its formative years, the Council relied on the generosity of its members and board of directors to meet its budgetary demands. This informality resulted in some lean years; in fact, in its first year, the NFTC ran a budget deficit of more than $600. Part of the reason for the shortfall was the question over how dues should be levied: should individuals and corporations pay the same, or should dues depend upon the size of the organization? Deciding on the latter, the Council set dues in the first year that varied from $100 to $1,500. Over time, a formal dues structure was installed, but financial woes dogged the Council. Forced to take out several loans, the Council at one point could not completely cover payroll. At the 1915 annual meeting, Willard Straight, the chairman of the finance committee, had to appeal to the board of directors to cover the budget deficit. Straight and Walter Clark loaned the Council $750 to fund Council activities for that year. [26] India House also made sizable grants to the NFTC annually at least until 1932.

Straight offered several potential solutions to make the Council's financial situation more sustainable. The committee suggested it could have the power to "call upon various members of the Council for a certain amount to be based upon publications received in the past year." Straight also said the Council should obtain pledges from members for multiple years. Receiving guarantees of support for three years would allow the Council to plan.[27]

The Council's budget increased slowly, reaching $50,000 by 1919. The conclusion of the conflict in Europe and the expansion of the Council allowed an expanded staff, but financial difficulties remained. The NFTC closed its budget deficit by decreasing salaries, contributing less to the operation of the convention, and increasing registration fees. The budget remained around $50,000 for several years, but the "sum the treasurer… [had] been able to raise in recent years has fallen short of the amounts approved by the annual meeting." Many members did not pay their promised dues, as the Council had only raised several thousand dollars per year more than when it had a much smaller membership. The chairman of the finance committee still did not think it was "desirable to put membership in the Council on a regular dues paying service." His solution was to expand membership in the Council to 100, with new members chosen from industries not currently represented.[28] The plan worked, and Council increased both membership and achieved budget stability.

With the newfound funds suddenly available in the operating budget, the Council focused anew on the mission of foreign trade education. It hired one Walter Hiatt, "an experienced publicity man," and undertook an extensive publicity campaign extolling the virtues and benefits of trade. Hiatt prepared a series of newspaper articles, all of which received wide circulation. He also prepared a series of articles demonstrating the importance of American imports entitled *"Things We*

Use." However, a subscription shortfall the following year forced the Council to lay off Hiatt and discontinue this aggressive campaign, as budget woes continued.[29]

NFTC chairman James Farrell pushed the Council to proclaim the importance of foreign trade to the nation. These educational efforts also allowed the NFTC to reach as many businesses as possible. While it always had large companies as part of its board of directors, the Council made conscious efforts to engage smaller firms. At the second foreign trade convention, held in 1915 in St. Louis, delegates focused on how smaller manufacturers could succeed as exporters. W.C. Downs, the United States commercial attaché to Australia, spoke about how small businesses could expand their overseas efforts. His practical lecture discussed what goods were suitable to export, how to bring goods to the attention of foreign buyers, and how to finance smaller transactions. He suggested American companies contact export commission houses, which had access to significant amounts of information and useful trade data.[30]

Foreign Trade Week

As part of its educational outreach, the Council also began to sponsor an innovative Foreign Trade Week during the 1920s. The NFTC worked with the U.S. Chamber of Commerce and other organizations to organize a blitz of educational events. Delegates gathered in New York for a week full of information about the vital nature of foreign trade to the American economy, with events also taking place throughout the country, including in high schools and colleges. The Council issued reports of the proceedings to newspapers around the nation. The Council planned the 1930 Foreign Trade Week to coincide with the San Francisco World's Fair, where it sponsored an exposition. The NFTC believed these events resulted in increased appreciation for the value and importance of foreign trade.[31]

Over time, Foreign Trade Week developed into a national event. By the beginning of the Second World War, even the federal government participated. The Bureau of Foreign and Domestic Commerce Activity distributed stickers and posters to children. The Council also printed National Foreign Trade Week posters to hang in post offices.

Foreign Trade Week was the largest of a number of activities intended to convince Americans about the virtues of foreign trade. One year an essay contest was organized for high school and college students in the interior of the country, to get them thinking about trade and maritime commerce. The contest theme was "the necessity of the merchant marine in order to develop foreign trade." Run by the NFTC's Committee on Education for Foreign Trade, contests took place at the University of Kansas, Harvard University, University of Wisconsin, and the University of Texas. The Education Committee also organized a similar contest for New York City high school students, which drew more than 100 entries.

THE WHITE HOUSE
WASHINGTON

October 3, 1942

My dear Mr. Farrell:

Again I welcome the opportunity to extend my cordial greetings to the National Foreign Trade Council and, on the occasion of its Twenty-ninth National Foreign Trade Convention, to congratulate the Council upon its record of achievement in promoting public understanding of the vital importance of international trade to this country and to the world.

Since I last greeted you, in 1941, our nation has been treacherously attacked by brutal aggressors who hate freedom. We have been forced into a desperate struggle for the preservation of a free world -- a struggle which demands every ounce of the effort of every one of us, on many fighting fronts, in production, and in getting the materials and the men where they are most needed. In that effort we do not, thank God, stand alone. The United Nations, and freedom-loving men everywhere, are going forward with us, shoulder-to-shoulder, to victory.

In a truly free world all men and all peoples must have certain rights. They must have the right to produce, to the fullest extent commensurate with their ability, the things which they are best able to produce. This means equality of access to materials and to capital. They must have the free choice of what they will produce, governed solely by sound economic principles and a due regard for the welfare of others. Each country must have the right to exchange its own products for things which it needs and wants and which other countries can produce to better advantage. In a free world no nation must be enslaved by any race, nation, or group which calls itself a master people and demands by force or aggression the fruits of another's labor, as is the announced intention of the Axis powers.

Not only must the forces of tyranny and conquest be overthrown and rendered impotent, but during the war and upon our victory we must build a world in which the rights of men -- all the rights of men -- shall be assured. This is a tremendous task.

The splendid work which the National Foreign Trade Council has done, and is doing, will help to establish a free world worthy of the sacrifice of our property, our labor, and our lives and of the property, labor, and lives of our valiant friends.

Very sincerely yours,

Franklin D. Roosevelt

Mr. James A. Farrell,
Chairman,
National Foreign Trade Council, Inc.,
26 Beaver Street,
New York, N. Y.

End of One Era, Dawn of Another

The NFTC underwent a transition beginning with its formal incorporation in 1938. As the institution grew larger, the board of directors decided legal incorporation would allow the Council to formalize institutional structures, elect officers and executive committees, and put it on firmer financial footing as a membership corporation.[32]

Around the same time, the increasing age of its founding chairman and longtime leader, James Farrell, reduced his ability to guide the organization he had nurtured for over thirty years. He died March 28, 1943, at his home on Fifth Avenue in New York, at the age of 80. Despite his infirmities, Farrell had remained active in the operation of the Council until his death, reviewing forthcoming publications, approving convention speakers, and offering advice from New York and his estate in Norwalk, Connecticut.

It is difficult to overstate Farrell's influence on the early years of the NFTC. Singlehandedly, he instituted many of the founding policies and priorities of the Council.[33] Indeed, his *New York Times* obituary placed great importance on his influence. After a cursory glance of his Horatio Alger story from day laborer to president of U.S. Steel, Farrell's obituary focused on his role as "Dean of Foreign Trade." Farrell was not only president of the largest corporation in the world, but he "broke all records for obtaining foreign orders for American goods." Farrell's retirement from U.S. Steel "meant no diminution of his interest and activities in the field of expanding the possibilities of his country's export business." The obituary went on to discuss, at length, his time as chairman of the NFTC. It noted how he worked for foreign trade principles that would ensure world peace and "break down the barriers of preferential trading systems."[34]

Despite the loss of James Farrell, the NFTC began to expand, especially after the end of World War Two. The organization transitioned from being almost a purely informative body to one which "implemented its determinations regarding the importance of foreign trade to the United States economy." The Allied victory presented opportunities and challenges. "Not since the first World War have foreign traders had thrust upon them so many problems of reconstruction and revitalization." The Council believed the end of the war would create an insatiable demand for American products since the war had destroyed European and Japanese trading abilities. In its 1945 annual letter to convention delegates, the NFTC reminded businessmen how it had helped the government during the war. Now, it had a similar obligation to "proffer advice and aid to Government in reorganizing and improving its peacetime equipment for promoting and protecting our foreign trade." The NFTC billed the 1945 convention as a unique opportunity for private enterprise to discuss steps needed for the economic reconstruction of the world.[35]

By the end of World War Two, the NFTC still retained its founding membership of manufacturers, bankers, and shippers; but had also broadened the scope of its membership to include importers, retailers, insurance firms, transportation companies, and the entire scope of foreign trade. The Council also had a much larger permanent staff and committee system that could respond to any future foreign trade problems. It was well-positioned for the challenges it would face in the post-war world.

Chapter Endnotes

[1] The building was constructed by the builder Richard Carman sometime after the fire of 1835, in the style of a Renaissance palazzo, residential palaces of Italian banking families. It was initially the home of the Hanover Bank which first purchased the property.

[2] "Downtown Business Men Organize to Foster Foreign Trade," *New York Times*, September 27, 1914.

[3] Ibid.

[4] James Farrell, "James Farrell to W. A. Mitchell", February 3, 1940, National Foreign Trade Council Records, Box 1.

[5] "Program, 27th National Foreign Trade Convention", July 1940, National Foreign Trade Council Records, Box 78, Folder 32.

[6] "Report of Third Annual Meeting, National Foreign Trade Council."

[7] "Program, 25th National Foreign Trade Convention", November 1938, National Foreign Trade Council Records, Box 78, Folder 30; "Documents Related to 29th Convention", n.d., National Foreign Trade Council Records, Box 78, Folder 34.

[8] "Program, 28th National Foreign Trade Convention," October 1941, National Foreign Trade Council Records, Box 78, Folder 33.

[9] "Program of Events, 17th National Foreign Trade Convention," May 1930, National Foreign Trade Council Records, Box 78, Folder 22.

[10] Ibid.

[11] Ibid.

[12] Magalhaes, "Report on the Twenty-Seventh National Foreign Trade Convention."

[13] "Program, 25th National Foreign Trade Convention."

[14] "Address of the Chairman and Reports of the Secretary and Treasurer of the National Foreign Trade Council", October 1929, National Foreign Trade Council Records, Box 24, Folder 12; "Program of Events, 17th National Foreign Trade Convention."

[15] "Program, 25th National Foreign Trade Convention."

[16] "Program of Events, 17th National Foreign Trade Convention."

[17] "Captain Robert Dollar Memorial Award", August 1978, National Foreign Trade Council Records, Box 112, Folder 1.

[18] Magalhaes, "Report on the Twenty-Seventh National Foreign Trade Convention."

[19] "Final Declaration of the Seventeenth National Foreign Trade Convention", May 1930, National Foreign Trade Council Records, Box 78, Folder 22.

[20] "Second Annual Meeting, The National Foreign Trade Council"; Finance Committee, "Invitation for Corporate Membership", 1938, National Foreign Trade Council Records, Box 24, Folder 7; "Minutes of Meeting of the Board of Directors of the NFTC", March 20, 1945, National Foreign Trade Council Records, Box 24, Folder 7.

[21] "U. S. Steel Rivals to Unite in Exports," *New York Times*, July 1, 1915.

[22] "Reports Delivered at the Sixth Annual Meeting of the National Foreign Trade Council", October 1919, National Foreign Trade Council Records, Box 24, Folder 11.

[23] Ibid.

[24] Ibid.

[25] Nitsan Chorev, *Remaking U.S. Trade Policy: From Protectionism to Globalization* (Ithaca: Cornell University Press, 2007), 46–47.

[26] "Second Annual Meeting, The National Foreign Trade Council."

[27] Ibid; "Report of Third Annual Meeting, National Foreign Trade Council."

[28] "Report of the Treasurer", November 8, 1918, National Foreign Trade Council Records, Box 24, Folder 10; "Reports of Chairmen, Secretary and Treasurer of the National Foreign Trade Council", October 1923, National Foreign Trade Council Records, Box 24, Folder 11.

[29] "Reports of Secretary and Treasurer of the National Foreign Trade Council", October 1924, National Foreign Trade Council Records, Box 24, Folder 11.

[30] NFTC, "How Smaller Manufacturers May Succeed as Exporters."

[31] "Address of the Chairman and Annual Reports of the National Foreign Trade Council", January 1936, National Foreign Trade Council Records, Box 24, Folder 12; "Final Declaration of the Twenty-Fifth National Foreign Trade Convention", November 1938, National Foreign Trade Council Records, Box 78, Folder 30; "Final Declaration of the Twenty-Second National Foreign Trade Convention", November 1935, National Foreign Trade Council Records, Box 78, Folder 37.

[32] "Address of the Chairman and Reports of the President and Treasurer of the National Foreign Trade Council", February 1934, National Foreign Trade Council Records, Box 24, Folder 12.

[33] "J.A. Farrell Dies; U.S. Steel Ex-head," *New York Times*, March 29, 1943.

[34] Ibid.

[35] "Preliminary Program, 32nd National Foreign Trade Convention", November 1945, National Foreign Trade Council Records, Box 78, Folder 37; "Awards Tell Trade History," *International Commerce,* October 31, 1966.

CHAPTER THREE

Challenging Protectionism, Defending International Business

AP/Life /Alfred Eisenstaedt

In the immediate postwar years, the National Foreign Trade Council continued to grow in size and stature, evolving from a largely informal group of exporters and their financiers, seeking ways to grow market share and educate the public on the importance of trade, into a set of large, often multinational companies looking to assist one another by sharing specialized economic information. American trade continued to expand early during this period, bringing economic prosperity to members of the NFTC. However, major difficulties began to spring up internationally in the 1960s and early 1970s, such as state seizure American private property, or onerous regulations on Americans trading or investing abroad. The war-weary world owed America and its private enterprises a great deal of money, and most creditors wanted it paid back in strong dollars. A growing balance of payments deficit placed certain sectors of the US economy in great peril. On the other hand, a weaker dollar fostered greater American exports. At the same time, the NFTC attracted a new breed of multinational companies as members. As a result, the NFTC membership became internally conflicted on many issues, though the fissures would not show for some time.

Presence at Bretton Woods

As government negotiators from around the world gathered at Bretton Woods to hammer out a post-war regime for regulating capital flows, exchange rates, and trade rules, the Council kept its members abreast through reports and bulletins. Members of the board, like Eugene Thomas and John Abbink, spent time at the conference talks in New Hampshire. They used these firsthand observations and other information to issue reports to its members and to form opinions about the accord. The Council thought a permanent international

THE WHITE HOUSE
WASHINGTON

October 22, 1945

My dear Mr. Thomas:

I shall be grateful if you will extend my greetings and best wishes to the delegates to the National Foreign Trade Convention.

The victory of the United Nations presents us with great and pressing problems of reorganization and reconstruction in all fields, but at the same time it gives the peoples of the world an unprecedented chance to remake their economic relations so as better to serve the common welfare.

Modern science and technology have placed enormous powers in our hands. For the first time in the long history of man it is technically possible to produce enough material goods so that all men everywhere may be adequately fed, decently housed, and comfortably clothed. The question is whether our arrangements for exchange and distribution will be such that these enormous productive powers are enabled to operate freely for the benefit of everyone.

We have that problem in the United States and we have it in the world. No one of us is wise enough to know all the measures that will be necessary to attain our goal. But we do know that the general direction must be to release energies and enterprise from the shackles that confine them -- shackles of ignorance, of private monopoly, or of excessive government control -- so that goods may be made and distributed, people fed, and jobs created. We shall not get forward toward freedom from want by placing new restrictions either upon production or exchange. On the contrary, we must reduce restrictions all around the circle; and we must try at the same time to promote stability and high employment.

Foreign trade is by definition international and the public measures that affect it ought therefore to be agreed on internationally whenever that is possible. The new international organizations now coming into existence, and in particular the Economic and Social Council of the United Nations, ought to be a great help to that end. The world is growing smaller every day and we shall need to live as good neighbors in a world of good neighbors if we hope to enjoy the prosperity which science and technology have brought within our power.

In all these matters the Government of the United States will continue to count on the advice and support of the American business community and in particular of the Foreign Trade Council. Your members, more than most of us, are actually engaged in practical international cooperation and their experience and wisdom, collected through the Council, have been and are of great help to the officers of the government charged with questions of international trade.

Very sincerely yours,

Harry Truman

Mr. E. P. Thomas,
President,
National Foreign Trade Council,
26 Beaver Street,
New York 4, N. Y.

institution where the heads of central banks could consult one another on monetary policy would benefit global trade. The International Monetary Fund's (IMF) proposed use of gold as a common currency denominator fit with the Council's longstanding belief in the advantages of sound money for international trade. As the initial details of the Bretton Woods agreement came together, the NFTC issued a statement calling for the IMF to receive unqualified support from policy-makers. The Council wanted the federal government to commit to a sizable subscription of funds to the IMF.[1]

The Marshall Plan and the Economic Cooperation Administration

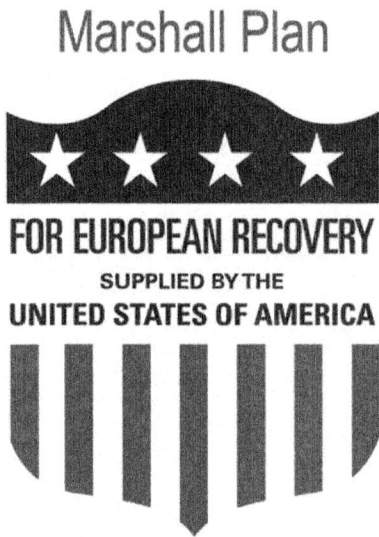

Marshall Plan

★ ★ ★ ★

FOR EUROPEAN RECOVERY

SUPPLIED BY THE

UNITED STATES OF AMERICA

After several years of fitful starts in the rebuilding of war-torn Europe, Secretary of State George Marshall emphasized the need for the United States to help return normal economic health to the world by aiding the reconstruction of Europe. He said there would be no lasting peace or political stability without a plan to encourage the emergence of political and social conditions in which free institutions can exist. The Marshall Plan was eventually allocated more than $12 billion, funds which were then transferred to European local governments, which used the aid to purchase food, fuel, and reconstruction materials from the United States. The plan established the Economic Cooperation Administration (ECA) to manage the reconstruction effort. The ECA stationed envoys, who were usually prominent businessmen, in every country to advise local governments on the optimal distribution of aid.

The ECA and the NFTC had a close relationship, and ECA Director Paul G. Hoffman won the Robert Dollar Memorial Award in 1950. The NFTC agreed that rebuilding the economies and infrastructure of Europe was vital to American security, and offering aid fit in with the Council's longstanding belief that foreign trade was not a zero-sum game. Expansion of international trade along liberal lines would benefit all parties. The Council believed the ECA had the potential to meet these lofty goals if it did not succumb to corruption or protectionist or ideological instincts. NFTC member companies had direct interests and input into how the Truman administration executed the ECA. Automobile and oil companies had branches in European nations, where they stood to benefit from reconstruction of local economies. And manufacturing members of the NFTC had the potential to profit directly when the ECA imposed a condition that certain manufactured goods had to come from American companies. When some European nations began using ECA funds to purchase goods from Latin America, the NFTC opposed these purchases.[2]

THE WHITE HOUSE
WASHINGTON

Augusta, Georgia
November 11, 1960

Dear Mr. Wolf:

It is a pleasure to send greetings to all attending the Forty-seventh National Foreign Trade Convention in New York City.

This year seems a particularly auspicious time to discuss the problems of foreign trade, since the United States is now engaged in several important programs which will affect international commerce. The United States, as a contracting party to the General Agreement on Tariffs and Trade, is now participating in a conference designed to increase international trade. We have entered these negotiations with a firm resolve to seek results which will benefit exporters, consumers and Americans in all walks of life. Negotiations on the external tariff of the European Economic Community, or Common Market, have already begun. I feel confident that, in spite of the difficulties and complexities, the outcome of these negotiations will be such as to make a real contribution to the expansion of free world trade.

Another of the Government's important economic programs is the export promotion program. A disturbing deficit in our balance of payments in 1958 and 1959 led to a concerted drive by the United States Government to encourage American businessmen to sell their products abroad. Although our exports have shown a definite upward trend this year, there is no room for complacency. We must continue to press American sales abroad in order to fulfill our responsibilities and maintain our position of strength in the world.

The activities of the National Foreign Trade Council have been important in promoting trade. And through trade its members are helping to advance the cause of peace in the world.

Sincerely,

Dwight D. Eisenhower

Mr. George W. Wolf, Chairman
National Foreign Trade Council
111 Broadway
New York 6, N. Y.

Public Recognition and Private Growing Pains

To outsiders of this era, NFTC presented a well-defined purpose and organizational structure. American business and government bodies recognized it as the voice of the American international business community. Symbolizing this growing stature, outside business groups began to use the NFTC's objective, expert analysis to promote their own goals and objectives. When several trade councils advertised the economic potential of Chile in the wake of efforts to stimulate industrial development, they relied upon values set by the NFTC to show how much capital could be re-exported to the United States at any time. The national media viewed the NFTC in the same fashion. On many occasions, the *New York Times* and the *Wall Street Journal* reprinted selections from Council publications verbatim.

One reason for the Council's continued sterling reputation was its contribution to sound commercial policies that moved toward a fairer and open system of trade. The Council continued to provide a forum for the exchange of ideas among "world-minded" business executives through conventions, board meetings, and publications. The NFTC also provided individual consultations with its members by brokering solutions to their specific international business problems. The board of directors, made up of nearly 100 company executives elected by membership of the entire Council, controlled NFTC operations and set priorities. Board members were company executives with experience in international operations, and committees served as a medium for the exchange of ideas. Country and area committees kept members abreast of economic and political developments throughout the world. Technical committees handled specialized business issues, such as customs drawbacks, foreign property, industrial property, industrial relations, insurance, international finance, and international public relations. Finally, the Council had special discussion groups for those concerned with balance of payments issues, international economic analysis, and war claims.[3]

The Council's decades of tireless work in trade promotion, trade education, and expanding export opportunities for U.S. businesses was officially recognized by the U.S government. In 1962, President Kennedy created the 'E' Awards Program to honor excellence in exporting (modeled on the 'E' Awards of World War Two, recognizing wartime production excellence.) It would be the nation's highest export honor. The very first set of 'E' Award honorees included the National Foreign Trade Council, who received the award from Secretary of Commerce Luther Hodges on Oct. 31 at the convention. Upon presentation of the award to Council president John Akin, Secretary Hodges remarked,

"I take great pleasure in presenting the National Foreign Trae Council an 'E' Award. The National Foreign Trade Council, Inc., a non-profit organization of businessmen, has worked assiduously for nearly a half century to educate American business and the public on the importance of overseas trade. It has developed various trade terms and definitions, compiled and published books and pamphlets on overseas trade and development, and worked with educational institutions to develop overseas business educations. This well-conceived program has been of material value to the economic growth and prosperity of the United States."

(Fifty two years later, on May 28, 2014, on the occasion of its Centennial birthday, Secretary of Commerce Penny Pritzker presented the NFTC with the "E Star" Award for its continued excellence in opening markets and supporting US exporters. She playfully remarked to NFTC President Bill Reinsch, "Next time don't wait fifty years!")

Despite the glowing and well-deserved accolade, however, the NFTC faced a series of internal difficulties. As American business changed, so did the composition of the Council. Many longtime domestic stalwarts of the Council left because of bankruptcy, merger, or disagreement with the anti-protectionist stance of the Council, causing a corresponding drop in dues revenue. Structurally, the Council had absorbed the staff and programs of its longtime partners the Council for Inter-American Cooperation (CIAC) including publication of its weekly *Noticias* reports, but this action did not add any new members

These membership and financial difficulties forced the Council to rethink some of its positions. Multinational corporations came to make up the bulk of the Council's more than 600 members, and they dominated its agenda. While this provided a global base of support for the Council, these members faced their own challenges. In the 1970s, large, international companies increasingly came under attack for acting unethically around the world. They were often accused of being bad for American business in particular and global business in general. The Council and its membership were experiencing dramatic growing pains— some of the worst of which occurred just 90 miles from America's shores.

November 16, 1963

Dear Mr. Hoglund:

I congratulate the National Foreign Trade Council for a half century of service to the nation's economy and send greetings and good wishes to those attending the Fiftieth National Foreign Trade Convention.

The merchants and manufacturers of America hold a proud place in our history and no group among them has enjoyed more esteem and admiration than the producers and traders responsible for our foreign commerce. Their service has enriched our nation, increased its material strength and deepened its ties with the rest of the world. It is not surprising that today, America looks to you and to your colleagues to sustain and enlarge the vital flow of goods from our shores to markets throughout the world.

Confident in your ability to uphold an unbroken tradition of enterprise and success in the international trading arena, the United States is now engaged in preparations for the most important tariff-cutting conference in history -- the sixth round of negotiations under the General Agreement on Tariffs and Trade. The outcome of these negotiations can be decisive to the future strength and the cohesiveness of the free world. It is our hope that the important preparatory talks now going on in Geneva will be fruitful and that soon our nation and others will be ready to negotiate on a comprehensive range of items -- a range that recognizes that trade is trade whether in manufactured products or harvested ones.

In carrying on these negotiations for the United States, our Special Representative for Trade Negotiations, Christian A. Herter, will need the help of the business community and other sectors of the economy. The final effect of the negotiations on the United States economy, however, will depend primarily on private producers and traders.

I am proud of the fact that my grandfather participated in the First National Foreign Trade Conference as Mayor of Boston. However, his comment of fifty years ago that "the awakening to modern export methods is not yet general enough" must be matched against the fact that today only five to ten percent of America's manufacturers are engaged in exporting. This situation must be improved and I look to the National Foreign Trade Council to help provide them leadership, enterprise, and enthusiasm needed to make the change quick and decisive.

With every good wish,

Sincerely,

Mr. E. S. Hoglund
Chairman
50th National Foreign Trade Convention
National Foreign Trade Council, Inc.
10 Rockefeller Plaza
New York 20, New York

NOTE:
E.S.H. Took original - NB

The Cuba Question

As the 1960's dawned, one of the main concerns for Council members was the protection of American property from state seizure. In the wake of expropriations in Cuba, South America, and Southeast Asia, the NFTC formed a committee to deal with the seizure of American property abroad. Nearly 100 of the Council's member companies had lost property in the Cuban expropriation, constituting the bulk of the nearly $861 million of privately owned property seized. The property-holders committee drafted a statement accusing the Cuban government of inflicting a serious setback to the entire system of free trade. The forceful tone of the statement was unusual for the NFTC, which usually refrained from strongly worded public statements in order to keep in the good graces of foreign governments. This time was different. The Council's Cuba statement read like an indictment. It accused the Fidel Castro government of shirking international laws, ignoring its domestic policies, and using threats and other coercive measures against individuals and companies.[4]

The actions of the Cuban government led the NFTC to conclude that economic relations with Cuba no longer made sense. While some members had already ceased trading with Cuba, the NFTC called for an immediate and complete embargo of Cuban goods. They believed continued trade would only continue benefiting a government opposed to free enterprise. In order to fix its economic relationship with the United States, the Cuban government needed to pay just compensation for expropriated property.[5] (Today, through its USA*Engage sanctions-focused program, the NFTC openly calls for an end to

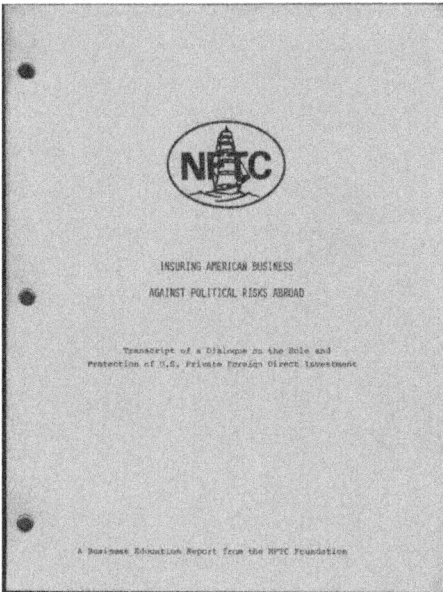

INSURING AMERICAN BUSINESS
AGAINST POLITICAL RISKS ABROAD

Transcript of a Dialogue on the Role and
Protection of U.S. Private Foreign Direct Investment

A Business Education Report from the NFTC Foundation

the embargo of Cuba. This is one of the extremely rare examples of the NFTC reversing a stance during its 100 year history.)

War Risk Insurance and Other Protections for Private Property

The Cuban revolution and 1962 missile crisis, as well as similar statist moves in other nations, spurred the NFTC to develop novel ways to protect members' overseas property. For instance, the missile crisis spurred interest among marine insurance underwriters to obtain better coverage before and during a possible war. The Council believed the system then in place would unnecessarily curtail exports during a crisis by limiting how much exporters could value their insured cargo. The NFTC successfully developed an alternative plan. In its scheme, commercial underwriters would continue to issue war risk insurance policies on competitive terms, but they would do so through the backing of a governmental reinsurance program. To gain access to this program and to ensure that it did not turn in to a government takeover of the insurance industry, the plan had private companies paying substantial premiums.[6]

The NFTC also lobbied Congress to protect the foreign property rights of American businesses based abroad. In 1966, the Council pushed the Senate to ratify an international convention for the settlement of investment disputes. The NFTC wanted America to join an international body called the International Centre for Settlement of Investment Disputes of the World Bank (ICSID) that would provide for the arbitration of disputes between governments and foreign investors.[7] The ICSID is one of the precursors to Investor-State Dispute Settlement (ISDS) jurisprudence of today. [8]

World Trade Dinner

Fiftieth

National Foreign Trade Convention

Wednesday, November twentieth

Nineteen hundred sixty-three

The Waldorf-Astoria

New York

ric Wyndham White
xecutive Secretary,
GATT............pg 4

William C. Wichman
Vice President,
General Electric Co...pg 7

Robert M. Norris
Pres., National Foreign
Trade Council.....pg 10

Luis Muñoz Marín
Governor
of Puerto Rico....pg 13

R. Sargent Shriver
Director,
The Peace Corps...pg 16

George D. Woods
President,
The World Bank....pg 20

50th National Foreign Trade Convention

National Foreign Trade Council, Inc.

November 18, 19, 20, 1963 • Waldorf-Astoria • New York City

Formerly
THE GENERAL ELECTRIC DEFENSE QUARTERLY

Volume VI • Number 4 • October–December 1963

Member Services

Besides the broad work of its many committees, the NFTC provided members with a wide range of business services. It gathered background information on specific problems of international business management. While fewer companies needed basic information about opening a branch or doing business in particular countries, the NFTC continued to provide members with vital, time-relevant information they would need to operate abroad.

The Council also helped to negotiate licensing agreements, making it easier for Americans to market goods abroad. On behalf of members as a whole and in individual circumstances, the NFTC connected businesses to influential politicians or lobbied for particular bills or business agreements.[9]

Birth of the International Human Resources (IHR) program

One of the major areas members sought the NFTC for advice was the salaries, benefits, and allowances American companies provided for overseas employees. In 1968, after several companies had requested this kind of information, the Council compiled a fairly detailed analysis of these questions based on ten overseas companies. With this baseline of information about compensation and benefits, the NFTC study showed the effects of changing allowances, like travel or housing benefits. This was the genesis of the Council's International Human Resources (IHR) program, still active today.

Many of the Council's multinational members had a similar international HR issue, but in reverse. Along with expatriate compensation, they also wrangled with the hiring of foreign talent to work in the United States. The NFTC collaborated with its member companies to expedite the immigration of trained foreign nationals. In 1965, the Hart-Celler Act replaced national-origin quotas with a single immigration cap.[10] This abolished the national origins quota system that was the essence of American immigration policy since the 1920s, replacing it with a preference system that focused on immigrants' family relationships with citizens or U.S. residents. Hart-Celler marked a radical break from the immigration policies of the past. Prior to the 1965 act, immigration policy specifically excluded Latin Americans, Asians and Africans, preferring northern and western Europeans over those from southern and eastern Europe.

Consequently, immigration dropped from Northern Europe and Canada (some of the very places American firms searched for talent), while total immigration soared. This increasing number of immigrants and the transition to a new immigration apparatus meant endless administrative headaches and delays for American businesses trying to hire foreign workers. On behalf of its members, the NFTC pushed for the easing of these delays, and it proposed a non-immigrant visa for foreign personnel with highly specialized knowledge or skills.[11] This became today's well-known H1B Visa.[12] In 1980, the Council was equally active on the issues of L-1 visa (intra-company transfer) processing and immigration reform.

International Tax Policy

Since the beginning of the Council, members had complained about what they said was unfair American tax policy. Americans trading abroad had their incomes taxed twice: in their country of operation and domestically. The NFTC encouraged the U.S. government to negotiate treaties that eliminated this double taxation. The closest it came to getting rid of double taxation was in the Eisenhower administration. The NFTC supported his attempts to lower the corporate tax rate on foreign income from foreign subsidiaries to 14 percentage points lower than the corporate rate on domestic income.[13]

The tax issue seemed to pop up whenever the American economy began to slow and tax collections decreased, and politicians began looking for additional revenue such as by ending tax exemptions for American companies trading abroad. For example, in 1961, at the beginning of the Kennedy Administration, the NFTC opposed efforts to classify some overseas ventures as foreign tax havens. Assistant Treasury Secretary for Tax Policy Stanley Surrey publicly stated that some corporations avoided corporate taxes by attributing their income to foreign sources, effectively sheltering them from the IRS. The NFTC argued that the flow of income to these overseas places was no greater than the flow of income from existing investments. Singling these ventures out would double tax American traders.[14]

Similarly, the NFTC lobbied Congress in the summer of 1963 for an exemption in Kennedy's proposed tax on foreign securities. It believed the law should exempt all foreign offerings related to the financing of exports and overseas businesses of American companies. Businesses undertook these kinds of transactions in the normal course of their business operations. Joseph Brady, Vice President of the Council's Tax Committee and a noted tax attorney, appeared before the House Ways and Means Committee arguing that routine sales to European Common Market countries would be subject to tax under the Administration's plan. Brady suggested an amendment to exempt any activity related to the active conduct of foreign trade.[15] These early forays gave the NFTC an indisputable expertise in international corporate tax policy that it still maintains today.

European Trade Issues, East and West

NFTC endorsement of American firms' interest in new trade opportunities in the Communist-bloc reflected the Council's commitment to open international

trade. Even with the solidification of Cold War relationships, the NFTC urged expansion of trade with the Soviet Union and the countries of Eastern Europe, a position it had staked out as early as the 1930's. In some ways, the NFTC helped to pave better relations and more frequent interactions between the United States and the Soviet Union. The Council began to hold panel discussions with members of the American and Soviet governments in the early 1970s. These discussions centered on the prospects of greater trade between the East and the West, particularly in the wake of the Six-Day War in 1967 and the Yom Kippur War in 1973. Officials in the American State Department had guarded views about the potential for greater trade, while the Soviets were more optimistic. At the Council luncheon, the head of a Soviet trade office pointed to the purchase of equipment for a large Soviet truck-manufacturing plant as an example of the potential for new trade endeavors.[16] This episode embodies of one of the Council's core beliefs - that peace, commercial ties, and mutual prosperity go hand in hand.

The NFTC also worked to repeal burdensome or onerous regulations on trade with the Eastern Bloc. As part of the Cold War guarding of America's strategic resources, the American government had restricted the export of certain technical and patent information through secrecy orders. As early as 1956, the NFTC asked the Department of Commerce to relax regulations on the export of technical data. It proposed that if the information contained in the patent application had not received a secrecy order within six months, then companies should be able to export without any clearance by the Department of Commerce.[17]

As far as trade with Western Europe was concerned, the NFTC viewed the administration's negotiating positons and tactics in the periodic General Agreement on Tariffs and Trade (GATT) negotiations as inadequate. As part of that agreement, countries periodically came together to add or subtract items from the list of goods not subject to tariffs. These broad-based international discussions departed from Cordell Hull's reciprocal trade agreements. Typically, staff and board members of the NFTC would attend these meetings to push for a greater number of goods not subject to duties. The Council, which had long been wary of the negative potential of the European Economic Community, thought the

THE WHITE HOUSE

WASHINGTON

October 16, 1966

I address this message to the National Foreign
Trade Convention on the eve of departing to
confer with the leaders of nations most directly
involved in the battle against aggression in
South Vietnam.

We seek a peaceful settlement of the struggle
and a base for social and economic development
in that restless part of the world.

These are universal objectives which I am
certain will preoccupy your own deliberations.

You are especially aware of the opportunity to
build a world of peace and prosperity through
expanded trade and investment among nations.

We in America must constantly encourage the
free flow of international commerce.

We are striving now to remove barriers to Free
World trade. We have taken steps to increase
trade with the Soviet Union and Eastern Europe.
We are working to speed the growth of developing
nations. And in all this, we rely upon continuing business-government cooperation to achieve
our goals.

You have my best personal wishes for a convention
that opens new pathways to peace through trade.

Lyndon B. Johnson

restrictive actions on the part of that group had clouded negotiations and prevented the further reduction of tariffs. In response to these lobbying efforts, Kennedy attempted to reassure the delegates to the 1963 foreign trade convention of his commitment to liberal trade policies. In the annual presidential letter to the 50th Convention, held just two days prior to his assassination , Kennedy noted how his grandfather, John F. Fitzgerald, had attended the first foreign trade convention. He told the Council that he would continue to push for lower tariff rates across all industries. Despite these public assurances, NFTC members privately doubted the likelihood of any major tariff reductions during the upcoming Round of GATT negotiations.[18]

The European trade integration, begun by the creation of the European Economic Community (EEC) in the 1957 Treaty of Rome, caused the U.S. to fear its own products would be shut out of the European market. For this reason, President Kennedy pressed for the passage of the Trade Expansion Act, which gave the President authority to decrease duties up to 50% from their 1962 levels or increase them up to 50% from their 1934 levels. Trade adjustment assistance was considered within the Act with several provisions that provided for the financial and technical assistance to firms and workers adversely affected by the opening of trade. It also made provisions for treating the European Economic Community for the first time as a single trade partner. After the act was passed, the Administration pressed for a new round of multilateral trade talks to utilize its new authority, which would become known as the Kennedy Round upon the death of President Kennedy in November 1963.

GATT Negotiations

The Kennedy Round officially opened in May of 1964 at the Palais des Nations in Geneva. It was the last GATT Round to have tariff reduction as its primary focus and the first Round to deal with non-tariff issues, such as dumping.[19] It also pioneered a "linear" style of negotiations. In contrast to the item-by-item negotiations of previous GATT Rounds, many countries offered across-the-board cuts of a certain percentage on all tariffs.

The moderate tariff reductions achieved by the close of the Kennedy Round in 1967 created new challenges for the NFTC. Balancing this success, some Council members, mainly from the chemical and steel industries, began to express greater fears of foreign competition. DuPont and the American Iron and Steel Institute both spoke out against President Johnson's inability to halt European actions that had placed American exports at a competitive disadvantage. European actions had included the erection of trade barriers, such as border taxes, import licensing requirements, and quotas. Because firms like DuPont and steel manufacturers were longtime members and directors of the NFTC, their position indicates there were tensions within the Council over which tariff reductions to support. Their loss of market share had led them to embrace these seemingly protectionist measures to protect American markets against foreign imports. While individual members of the NFTC spoke out against this GATT tariff lowering, Donald Heatherington, Vice President of the Council, publicly expressed satisfaction with lowered tariffs.[20]

After the conclusion of the Kennedy Round of tariff cutting, steel, textile, chemical and other commodity companies involved with the NFTC expressed fears over the next round of GATT negotiations, to be held in Geneva. These sectors, all imperiled by foreign imports, believed that the resultant 35 percent cut in tariffs on certain items would flood the American market with cheap goods. These protests reached a boiling point when representatives of oil, steel, meat, and chemical companies testified in front of the Senate Finance Committee to support quotas on foreign imports in their industries. Appearing opposite these representatives were members of President Johnson's cabinet and NFTC staff members. NFTC representatives argued that quotas would set off retaliatory actions. To attempt to quell these protectionist efforts, the Johnson Administration sent Special Trade Representative William Roth[21] to speak at the National Foreign Trade Convention in support of the ongoing GATT negotiations.[22]

Balance of Payments Crisis

The protectionist moves by some companies and members of Congress related to a significant development in American international finance during the 1960s and 1970s: the balance of payments crisis. The payments balance represented receipts and disbursements of all public and private international transactions. Transactions included trade, as well as foreign aid, military expenditures, and travel by citizens. The NFTC typically wanted America to have a positive payments balance. As a group of exporters, this signaled a healthy outflow of goods and since capital was not leaving the country, a positive payments balance meant a stronger dollar.

Historical data maintained by the NFTC's balance of payments committee showed that America had begun to run a balance of payments deficit during the late 1950s. This deficit had a number of causes: European economies had begun to recover from the Second World War; Asian economies began to develop; the American economy became more specialized; and American consumers acquired a voracious appetite for overseas products.[23] The deficit fluctuated, but the trend line was in the negative direction, never dropping below $1.2 billion. The NFTC opposed any attempts to remedy the payments deficit through restrictions on long-term private investment. It believed there was no painless solution to the crisis.

The persistent imbalance and outflow of dollars led to consistent speculation that the Federal Government would tighten its monetary policy. Both imports and exports continued to rise, breaking previous records and resulting in a net trade surplus during much of the 1960s. This gain in exports could largely be attributed to steel, aircraft, fats and oils, raw cotton, and scrap metal. The NFTC saw exports as a way to reduce the balance of payments deficit. Rather than placing quotas or other barriers on imports, it wanted the government to focus on increasing exports. The NFTC maintained that record imports were actually a sign of a healthy economy, as consumers bought more foreign products.[24]

The balance of payments crisis resulted in President Nixon taking the United States off the gold standard in 1971, effectively ending the Bretton Woods Agreement. The NFTC had long supported a strong dollar, but by this point, the Council's membership included a significant number of multinational corporations. These members had more flexible stances on the value of the dollar. Some Council members sought advice from the staff of the NFTC about how ending the direct convertibility of the dollar to gold would affect their international operations.[25]

THE WHITE HOUSE

WASHINGTON

November 3, 1972

As the members of the National Foreign Trade Council
meet to deliberate the issues and challenges facing
international business, the United States stands at the
threshold of an unprecedented era of peace and prosperity through world trade.

Our new relationships with the Soviet Union and the
People's Republic of China and our initiatives on behalf
of a more open and equitable world trading system are
revitalizing our competitive spirit in the world marketplace.

We must now work together to use the new opportunities
we have created to bring about a substantial growth in
our country's exports and to provide for a trade policy
that will serve all of our national trade needs in the
years ahead.

As members of an organization that is directly concerned
with international trade and investment, you are in the
vanguard of those who recognize the need to bring about
the conditions that will help us attain these objectives in
the years ahead.

The experience that derives from your more than five
decades of service to America's international commerce
is a source of sustaining strength for a nation that more
than ever depends on your constructive contributions in
this vital area.

I wish you every success at these deliberations and
throughout the year ahead.

Richard Nixon

Nixon-era Economic Policy

Nixon's plans to increase foreign trade and ameliorate the payments deficit received the support of the NFTC. A new trading mechanism called DISCs[26] was created to allow companies to defer income from exports, provided that income was settled through this system. Once accumulated, income would be paid to the parent company as a dividend. The parent company would report the income, with a credit allowed for any appropriate foreign taxes. Parent companies could also borrow funds from their DISCs without realizing taxable income. The Council testified before Congress in support of the proposal, helping its passage, albeit in a weaker form than it would have liked.[27]

The NFTC opposed several aspects of the Nixon Administration's economic policy, such as a job development tax credit. This credit would have given tax exemptions to machinery and equipment if purchased from American suppliers, which deviated from market-based principles.

The NFTC also faced a problem of what to do when the Nixon Administration placed a 10 percent surcharge on imports of most manufactured articles. Importers were stunned. The NFTC reacted more cautiously since exporters made up the bulk of its membership. It did not yet know if previously enacted anti-inflationary price freezes would allow importers to pass on the extra charges to consumers. However, Robert Norris, the President of the NFTC, expressed some support for the President's actions as part of a set of comprehensive measures to strengthen America's competitive position in world trade by strengthening the value of the dollar.[28]

The complexity of the balance of payments crisis and manufactured goods surcharge were mere precursors to a wave of trade and macroeconomic issues awaiting the NFTC, its member companies, and the nation, in the 1970's. While the Council would weather the storm, it would emerge as a changed organization.

Chapter Endnotes

[1] "NFTC Board Meetings, 1948"; National Foreign Trade Council, "Summary of Current Work," 1945, National Foreign Trade Council Records, Box 24, Folder 18; "Minutes of Meeting of the Board of Directors of the NFTC"; "Bretton Woods Agreement" (National Foreign Trade Council, March 21, 1945), National Foreign Trade Council Records, Box 130, Folder 13.

[2] "Minutes of Meeting of the Board of Directors of the NFTC," March 20, 1945, National Foreign Trade Council Records, Box 24, Folder 7; "NFTC Board Meetings, 1947" (National Foreign Trade Council, Inc., 1947), National Foreign Trade Council Records, Box 2; "NFTC Board Meetings, 1948"; National Foreign Trade Council, INC., "The Record for 1948", 1949, National Foreign Trade Council Records, Box 24, Folder 14; "Report on the Thirty-Eighth National Foreign Trade Convention"; National Foreign Trade Council, INC., "The Record for 1952,",February 1953, National Foreign Trade Council Records, Box 24, Folder 14; National Foreign Trade Council, "The Record for 1953," February 1954, National Foreign Trade Council Records, Box 24, Folder 14, .

[3] "NFTC Membership Services" (National Foreign Trade Council, Inc., 1962), National Foreign Trade Council Records, Box 77, Folder 10.

[4] "U.S. Group Formed Against Seizures," *New York Times*, July 8, 1960; "Deep Hurt to Trade Charged to Actions of Castro's Regime," *New York Times*, October 25, 1960; "Final Declaration of the Forty-Seventh National Foreign Trade Convention," November 1960, National Foreign Trade Council Records, Box 80, Folder 52, ; Brendan Jones, "Parley to Study U.S. World Trade," *New York Times*, November 13, 1960; National Foreign Trade Council, "The Record for 1960," 1961, National Foreign Trade Council Records, Box 24, Folder 15.

[5] National Foreign Trade Council, "The Record for 1961", 1962, National Foreign Trade Council Records, Box 24, Folder 15.

[6] "Loss of Exports in Crisis Feared," *New York Times*, October 29, 1962.

[7] "Investment Treaty Is Urged by Foreign Trade Council," *New York Times*, March 10, 1966.

[8] While the Investor-State Dispute Settlement Instrument [ISDS] is often associated with arbitration under the rules of ICSID, the ISDS in fact often takes place under the auspices of international arbitral tribunals governed by different rules and/or institutions, such as the London Court of International Arbitration, the International Chamber of Commerce, the Hong Kong International Arbitration Centre or the UNCITRAL Arbitration Rules.

[9] "NFTC Membership Services"; "NFTC Board Meetings, 1968" (National Foreign Trade Council, 1968), National Foreign Trade Council Records, Box 5; "NFTC Board Meetings, 1974" (National Foreign Trade Council, 1974), National Foreign Trade Council Records, Box 6; "Management," *New York Times*, July 30, 1976.

[10] The Immigration and Nationality Act of 1965 (Pub.L. 89–236, 79 Stat. 911, enacted June 30, 1968), also known as the Hart–Celler Act, abolished the National Origins Formula that had been in place in the United States since the Emergency Quota Act. It was proposed by Representative Emanuel Celler of New York, co-sponsored by Senator Philip Hart of Michigan, and promoted by Senator Edward Kennedy of Massachusetts.

[11] "NFTC Board Meetings, 1969" (National Foreign Trade Council, 1969), National Foreign Trade Council Records, Box 5; "Easing of U.S. Visas Asked for Key Corporate Visitors," *New York Times*, October 24, 1969; "NFTC Board Meetings, 1972" (National Foreign Trade Council,1972), National Foreign Trade Council Records, Box 5.

[12] The H-1B is a non-immigrant visa in the United States under the Hart-Cellar 1965 Immigration and Nationality Act. It allows U.S. employers temporarily to employ foreign workers in specialty occupations. If a foreign worker in H-1B status quits or is dismissed from the sponsoring employer, the worker must either apply for and be granted a change of status to another non-immigrant status, find another employer (subject to application for adjustment of status and/or change of visa), or leave the U.S.

[13] "Final Declaration of the Thirty-Second National Foreign Trade Convention", November 1945, Box 78 Folder 37; "The Booklet Offers a Summary of Council Activities for the Preceding Year." n.d.; "Final Declaration of the Thirty-Fourth National Foreign Trade Convention"; National Foreign Trade Council., "The Record for 1951", 1952, National Foreign Trade Council Records, Box 24, Folder 14.

[14] "Users of 'Tax Havens' Abroad Batten Down for Political Gale," *New York Times*, February 26, 1961.

[15] "Exporters Seek Tax Exemptions," *New York Times*, August 23, 1963.

[16] "U.S. Trade Policy Arouses Optimism," *New York Times*, November 26, 1966; "Russian and Aide of U.S. Differ on Ties," *New York Times*, November 15, 1973.

[17] National Foreign Trade Council, "The Record for 1955."

[18] "Foreign Traders Doubt Success of Kennedy Tariff Negotiations," *New York Times*, November 21, 1963.

[19] "Dumping" is a practice whereby a company exports a product at a price lower than the price it charges in its home market and thereby causes injury to a competitor in the country receiving the exports.

[20] "Industries in U.S. Assail Tariff Cut," *New York Times*, May 17, 1967.

[21] William M. Roth, not to be confused with Delaware Senator William V. Roth.

[22] "Confusion Noted by Both Sides," *New York Times*, October 29, 1967.

[23] Ibid.

[24] "Export Rise Seen by Trade Council," *New York Times*, January 26, 1961; "10% Rise in Trade Forecast for '66," *New York Times*, February 1, 1966.

[25] "Council Decries Lag in Move to Freer World Markets"; "NFTC Board Meetings, 1971" (National Foreign Trade Council, 1971), National Foreign Trade Council Records, Box 5.

[26] Domestic International Sales Corporation

[27] "NFTC Board Meetings, 1971"; "Export Total Expected to Set Record in '73 Despite Barriers," *New York Times*, January 2, 1973; "NFTC Board Meetings, 1974."

[28] "NFTC Board Meetings, 1971"; "Issue and Debate," *New York Times*, April 7, 1975; "Trade Group Backs Investment Abroad," *New York Times*, January 3, 1972; "Sudden 10% Surcharge Is Assailed by Importers," *New York Times*, August 17, 1971.

CHAPTER FOUR

Turmoil and Crossroads

The turmoil of the 1970's—inflation, unemployment, the energy crisis, Cold War maneuverings, and on the trade front, a massive trade deficit and major legislative changes- represented both crisis and opportunity for the NFTC. By weighing in on the important issues of the day, it attracted new multinational members. This in turn led to the need to defend multi-nationals in the court of public opinion, which the NFTC did vociferously. Internally, there was a changing of the guard, with the retirement of several longtime leaders and staff members.

The Trade Act of 1974

President Ford signing the Trade Act of 1974. Future NFTC Chairman Alan Wolff can be seen on the left; he was STR General Counsel at this time.

In reaction to the payments crisis, inflationary pressures, and discriminatory trading practices, a bill which ultimately became the Trade Act of 1974 gave the President the power to negotiate unilaterally the lowering of tariff barriers. This gave the White House flexibility to deal with excessively rapid increases in imports and unfair domestic and international cooperation - i.e. safeguards. The President would also be able to grant "most favored nation" (MFN) status to trading partners, and established a system of generalized trading preferences for developing countries. The Council saw, in the law, potential to eliminate tariffs altogether. While there was already a relatively low tariff on many goods, some items for one reason or another still had higher rates. The NFTC wanted to modify the proposal to empower the President to reduce or eliminate duties altogether.[1]

The legislation was so important that the Council held a special Board meeting in May 1973, where directors made line-by-line comments about the act. The Council had solicited comments from its members, and the biggest issue surrounded the nearly unilateral power that the President would get to change tariff rates. While the NFTC favored this kind of flexibility, leaders thought there should be some limit. The Council also wanted the bill to involve private industry more in creating foreign trade legislation and regulation. It believed the President should be encouraged to consult with private industry through an informal council. Part of this consultation should include creating a tariff commission made up of private business leaders. When a major market event took place, the commission would meet to discuss what policies should be taken, and then it would advise the President.[2] Today, the President's Export Council fills this role, with the participation of many NFTC member companies.

The passage of the Trade Act of 1974 was a seminal moment in American trade policy. The act helped industry in the United States become more competitive and phase workers into more globally competitive industries or occupations. It created "fast track" authority for the President to negotiate trade agreements that Congress can approve or disapprove but cannot amend or filibuster. It also gave the President broad authority to counteract injurious and unfair foreign trade practices. Section 201 of the Act required the International Trade Commission to investigate petitions filed by domestic industries or workers claiming injury or threat of injury due to expanding imports. If such injury was found, restrictive measures could be implemented. Section 301 was designed to eliminate unfair foreign trade practices that adversely affect U.S. trade and investment in both goods and services. Under Section 301, the President must determine whether the alleged practices are unjustifiable, unreasonable, or discriminatory and burden or restrict U.S. commerce. If the President determines that action is necessary, the law directs that all appropriate and feasible action within the President's power should be taken to secure the elimination of the practice.

The act also contained the Jackson-Vanik Amendment denying MFN status to certain countries with non-market economies that restrict emigration, but giving the President authority to grant a yearly waiver of its application to individual countries. The NFTC wanted to increase exports and imports by extending bilateral commercial agreements with several non-market economies. With the opening of the China trade following Nixon's visit there, the Council endorsed a proposal to exempt China from provisions of the amendment.

The Energy Crisis

While capital outflows and military expenditures associated with the Vietnam conflict continued to increase the payments deficit, it was the actions of the Organization of Petroleum Exporting Countries (OPEC) that created the most damage. By the middle of the 1970s, the cost of imported petroleum accounted for nearly the entire deficit. By this point, several energy concerns were members of the NFTC, and they wanted to find ways around the Middle East's stranglehold on the American energy market through open expansionist solutions. At the 60th annual convention, the Council appealed to all energy-importing nations to seek joint solutions and to avoid destructive competition for the available supplies of oil and gas. Council members called on industrialized nations to help oil-producing nations diversify their industries. Wealthier nations should invest their surplus capital in energy-hungry nations, and they should coordinate national energy research programs in order to avoid destructive competition, the Council concluded.[3]

THE WHITE HOUSE

WASHINGTON

November 14, 1975

My warmest greetings to the delegates and distinguished guests at the Sixty-Second National Foreign
Trade Convention.

Your convention theme indicates your traditional de-
votion of time and talent to the pressing issues and
prospects of world trade and investment. It also con-
firms that your membership stands ready, as always,
to serve the national interest by bringing fresh insight
to matters of critical public concern.

Energy and food shortages, inflation and recession
have brought serious economic challenges to Americans
and to the entire world community. Unless we face
these challenges cooperatively and constructively, we
jeopardize international relations that have taken us a
generation to build. As the vanguard of the world trade
movement in this country, you can immeasurably contribute toward the kind of international economic climate that will benefit people everywhere.

You have my very best wishes for every success at
these sessions and in the coming year.

Gerald R. Ford

In Defense of Multinational Corporations

The international energy crisis, a stagnating American economy, and a changing membership base, placed the NFTC and its members in a difficult position. As noted above, the NFTC membership had slowly evolved during the prior decade. While it had been founded as an organization of exporters, shippers, steel interests, and manufacturers, multinational firms now began to steer the organization. These included international investment banking firms and other multinational conglomerates. As it shifted to these more globalized corporations, the NFTC became a staunch defender of their legitimacy during a period when they attracted intense, often politically motivated criticism.

Labor unions were one source of attacks, citing multinationals for poor labor practices and exporting jobs. Multinationals looked to the NFTC to defend them. In a survey of more than 40 multinational companies of foreign traders and investors, the Council found no evidence to support the contention that foreign production had reduced exports or domestic employment. This publication, "*The Impact of United States Foreign Direct Investment on United States Employment and Trade*," countered claims of organized labor and academics that foreign direct investment had a deleterious effect on American jobs. Research performed by the staff of the Council found that American companies abroad sold more than double the amount of goods from overseas plants as they exported in manufactured goods. The study did strike a pessimistic note, however. Because of broader economic difficulties, the NFTC worried about the rise of protectionist legislation, such as the loss of tax incentives for foreign affiliates, controls on capital outflows, restrictions on the export of industrial technology, and the establishment of a governmental agency to control imports.[4]

In September 1975, Council President Robert Norris gave a highly anticipated speech to the International Advertising Association outlining in detail the NFTC's positions in defense of multinational corporations. He said the Council was deeply concerned about the criticisms and attacks on global companies. While he admitted these companies needed to refocus efforts on complying with local regulations, critics had gone too far in questioning the fundamental right of multinational corporations to "operate and, by making a profit, to survive and to promote economic growth for the immediate benefit of employees, shareholders, customers, and tax-receiving governments as well as for the long-range benefit of the world economy."[5]

He reviewed the history of criticisms mounted against multinationals, beginning with charges in 1972 that corporations had intervened in Chilean national elections. These charges led to a UN investigation and the convening of the Senate Foreign Relations Subcommittee on Multinational Corporations. The subcommittee recommended making it a criminal offense for American citizens to make contributions to a government agency or officer to influence a foreign election, which led to the passage of the Foreign Corrupt Practices Act in 1977. [6] The NFTC and its multinational members actually supported the passage of the act, because, in the long run, FCPA protected U.S. companies from the pressure to engage in corrupt activities.

Norris and the NFTC argued these and similar events demonstrated the need for balance in the historical record of multinational corporations. He cited a study by the Commerce Department showing how total employment of 298 multinationals expanded at a rate of 1 and 1/2 times faster than total domestic employment of all private industry in the same period. Few plants had actually moved abroad. Those that did came from a small number of industrial sectors, components, and raw materials. The rapid growth of U.S. imports in recent years was attributable not to American multinational firms, but to the products of German, Japanese, and other foreign producers who entered the American market without ties to American corporations.[7]

Multinationals also did not export capital, Norris continued. The sum of balance of payments inflows from foreign direct investments between 1965 and 1974 was more than twice the sum of outflows for new direct investment abroad. Nor did multinationals exploit the economies of host countries. Instead, the NFTC thought of them as "engines of development." Foreign direct investment (FDI) brings managerial know-how, better methods of production, and better products for the market. Further, much of a host country's exports come from these investments, and local taxes paid by foreign investors enabled host countries to meet their own fiscal responsibilities. These companies employed local labor, encouraged exploration and development of raw materials, expanded jobs, and led to a better overall standard of living.[8]

The work of multinationals also did not cause the currency crisis or the balance of payments deficit. The NFTC argued that exhaustive studies showed that multinationals participate only tangentially in this process, while the root cause of the problem was the failure of governments to heed changing exchange rates. Norris cited surveys and reports conducted for the Senate Subcommittee on Multinationals demonstrating how American multinationals did not use the forward market or the banking sector to place short-term hedges against the devaluation of the dollar in early 1973.[9]

Finally, Norris and the NFTC argued that multinationals did not evade taxes. Critics contended that multinationals manipulated transfer prices of intracompany transactions (transfer pricing) to minimize profits in high-tax countries and to maximize profits in lower-tax countries. The NFTC countered that multinationals did not have this kind of freedom, because governments severely scrutinize these transactions in the interest of maximizing their own tax revenue. Put simply, governments worldwide already paid enough attention to transfer pricing actions.[10]

Norris concluded his 1975 speech by conceding that not all international companies were innocent of questionable activities. Some investigations had merit, and some domestic legislation could improve international business arrangements. Overall, though, critics seemed to simply object to the "bigness" of international corporations. They wanted to "return to a time when the world's work was carried on by small companies, small retail stores…and small governments." These misguided and emotionally charged attacks on multinational corporations precluded a balanced examination of their role in the world's economic development. The NFTC led the business community in answering these charges and shared the facts about multinational corporations to audiences throughout the world.[11]

The Burke-Hartke Bill

One legislative attack on multinationals was the Burke-Hartke bill, which would drastically curb the export of capital through tax changes and other restrictions, while also installing import quotas based on the average historical import volumes of the period 1965 to 1968. Pegging quotas to these dates would result in a substantial drop in imports. The bill would also eliminate tax credits on income earned abroad and forced business to count taxes in the year they were earned, rather than allowing companies to repatriate them later through the DISC (formerly known as FSC) mechanism.

NFTC members vociferously opposed the bill. Robert Norris railed against the legislation at the San Francisco Area World Trade Association, warning that the bill would return the country to the disastrous policies of the Smoot-Hawley era. Norris and the NFTC believed the government needed to return to policies of industrial growth and expanded trade.[12] To strengthen opposition to the bill, the NFTC submitted an expert analysis of the tax increases that it hoped would sway members of Congress and the press.

The Council's main objections were the limitation on the use of the foreign tax credit, the repeal of DISC, taxation on undistributed foreign earnings, and the repeal of allowances for oil, gas, and mineral production. The Council believed that repealing the use of foreign tax credits would unfairly single out American businesses operating abroad, resulting in double taxation. There would also be negative consequences to American shareholders in taxing the earnings of foreign affiliates, which would likely lead foreign governments to level retaliatory taxes on American companies.[13] The Burke-Hartke Bill was never passed, but it set the terms of the trade debate for over half a decade.

Another trend of the 1970's were widespread fears of foreigners taking over American businesses, such as when Iran sought to buy a large share of Pan American Airlines, and other Arab nations moved to purchase real estate and bank holdings. In response, New Jersey Senator Harrison Williams proposed a bill in early 1975 restricting foreign investment, particularly related to corporate takeovers and large inflows of petrodollars. The bill would have amended the Securities Exchange Act to require disclosure of ownership of stock in public corporations. Foreign investors wanting to acquire more than five percent of an American company would have to give 30-day notices to the SEC. The President would also have the power to bar any foreign investment exceeding five percent ownership of any domestic company with assets of more than $1 million. The NFTC opposed Williams' bill because of the potential retaliatory measures from foreign nations.[14]

Changing with the Times

In addition to these external issues, the NFTC faced a series of internal transitions during this era, which began years earlier with William Swingle's retirement in February 1962. Swingle had served as President since 1950, working for the Council since 1938. To succeed him, the board named John Akin president.

The summer of 1962 also saw the death of George Wolf, Chairman of the NFTC since 1956. Wolf was a former executive in General Motors' overseas operation and the retired president of U.S. Steel Export, continuing the long connection between U.S. Steel and the NFTC. Notably, Wolf had received the Captain Robert Dollar Memorial Award in 1955.

Unfortunately, Akin died just a few months after Wolf, leaving the Council with no permanent President or Chairman. James Farrell, Jr. agreed to serve as Temporary Chairman while the Council searched for new leadership. The younger Farrell was the son of the first Chairman of the NFTC, and he also headed U.S. Lines, a shipping company specializing in the African trade.

After several months of searching, the Board of Directors named E.S. Hoglund as Chairman and Robert Norris as president. Norris was the Vice President of RCA International, based in Rome. He directed the commercial operations of the company's joint venture with the Istituto per la Ricostruzione Industriale. Norris also had worked with the Lederle Laboratories Division of American Cynamid. Hoglund, a former executive of GM, served as Chairman for seven years before Robert Dixson, a retired President of Johnson & Johnson, succeeded him. Dixson had played a major role in expanding the manufacturing, distribution and sales of products for Johnson & Johnson, and he served as a board member of the Far East-America Council of Commerce and Industry and an adviser to the Export-Import Bank of the United States.

NFTC Chairman Robert Dixson, President of Johnson & Johnson, receiving the 1972 Captain Robert Dollar Memorial Award for his career achievements in the promotion of international trade. Presenting the award is Henry Parker.

The latter half of the 1970s saw yet another wave of leadership changes at the NFTC. Dixson resigned in January 1976 after seven years as Chairman. The Board replaced him with James Roche. Roche was the former Chairman and CEO of GM. He had keynoted the national foreign trade convention, and he had a long association with the Council, particularly during the 1960s. Roche resigned after two years, and Kenneth Jamieson, former Chairman and CEO of Exxon, became Chairman of the NFTC in 1979. Meanwhile, James Farrell, Jr., who had first joined the Board of Directors in 1946, died in 1978, the same year that Robert Norris retired as President, with the Board naming Richard Roberts as his successor in 1979.

The 1970s also saw major changes in the personnel of the nearly 40-person Council staff. Several long-time staffers retired. One of these, Helene Bienzle, had joined the NFTC in September 1931. She worked on a variety of projects, most notably coordinating the foreign trade convention's World Trade Dinner and serving as Council Secretary, before retiring in January 1974.

Financially, the NFTC faced several lean years in the late 1970s. Membership dues and convention receipts slowed, and, for the first time, attendance at a foreign trade convention declined in 1974. For the Council, the conventions had long funded most other activities. The recession, political turmoil surrounding Watergate, and disruptions related to increased security measures at the Waldorf-Astoria led many businesses to forgo sending delegates to the annual meeting of foreign traders. Companies no longer sent as many delegates to the conventions, and trade groups such as the Bankers' Association began to hold their meetings separately from the convention. The Council tried to reinvigorate the conventions by adding corporate memberships, so attendees would each not have to purchase individual memberships. It moved the publication of the convention's annual declaration to the opening press conference to maximize press attention. It also moved away from offering a wide swath of topics to focusing on fewer topics in greater depth – a 'breadth or depth' tension with which the Council still struggles today.

As the NFTC transitioned away from multi-day conventions, it began to hold regular seminars and luncheons with influential political business leaders. These gatherings provided members with access to the Council's expertise and put businesses in touch with foreign politicians and officials hoping to lure American business. These meetings and briefings with US and foreign officials remain a mainstay of the Council's activities.

In response to the changing economic circumstances, global trade patterns, and the dynamics and operations of the NFTC, one of Roberts' first acts as President was the creation of the National Foreign Trade Council Foundation in June 1979. The Foundation would be a nonprofit educational institution to carry out the educational functions of the Council and plan and operate the convention. Additionally, this educational arm would issue information on careers in foreign trade and organize foreign trade statistics. Its tax-exempt legal status would allow it to receive tax-deductible grants for research into international trade, investment, and economic matters.

As the 1970's came to a close, the NFTC was at a crossroads. The attraction of protectionism among firms affected by global competition had led to defections from companies and sometimes entire sectors that had long supported the Council's work and policy priorities. Criticism of the multinational firms placed the NFTC in a defensive posture against legislation that would have curtailed the open trading regime its members favored. Internal structural, financial and personnel challenges continued to arise. But the organization would respond vigorously to these challenges after 1980, forging new directions, and re-asserting itself as the principal voice for American business on international trade.

Chapter Endnotes

[1] "NFTC Board Meetings, 1973" (National Foreign Trade Council, 1973), National Foreign Trade Council Records, Box 5; "Export Total Expected to Set Record in '73 Despite Barriers"; "Limited Impact Seen on Imports," *New York Times*, February 14, 1973.

[2] "NFTC Board Meetings, 1973."

[3] "10% Rise in Trade Forecast for '66"; "Export Rise Seen by Trade Council"; "Gains Predicted in U.S. Payments," *New York Times* January 23, 1964; "Joint Solution on Energy Is Urged by International Businessmen," *New York Times*, November 14, 1973; "NFTC Board Meetings, 1975" (National Foreign Trade Council, 1975), National Foreign Trade Council Records, Box 6.

[4] "NFTC Board Meetings, 1972"; "Limited Impact Seen on Imports," *New York Times* Feb. 14, 1973. .

[5] "NFTC Board Meetings, 1975."

[6] Ibid.

[7] Ibid.

[8] Ibid.

[9] Ibid.

[10] Ibid.

[11] Ibid.

[12] "NFTC Board Meetings, 1972."

[13] Ibid; "NFTC Board Meetings, 1979" (National Foreign Trade Council, 1979), National Foreign Trade Council Records, Box 6.

[14] Ibid; "Issue and Debate."

CHAPTER FIVE

Impact in Washington

The NFTC had always advocated for open, rules-based trading, but during its first 60 years it rarely engaged in direct political lobbying. However, global economic and political events were making this position increasingly untenable. As the world's economy and businesses became more globalized, governments around the world began to exert more control over trade policy. Rising government control, protectionist impulses, and politicization of the economy forced the NFTC to change. Quickening this shift, and fashioning its contours, was a series of developments that opened up new opportunities for the NFTC. After careful initial steps, the NFTC became an organization whose major purpose was the full-throated defense of free trade principles through active lobbying in Washington.

Beginning the Slow Move to Washington

Deindustrialization and the near-collapse of certain sectors of the industrial economy continued to create protectionist pressures within the United States. In the early 1980s, the NFTC pushed back against a proposed mandate that would have required that a certain percentage of automobile parts be produced in America or Canada. The NFTC argued this policy would not save jobs, and would invite retaliation, which, in turn, would actually lead to fewer jobs. What was significant about the NFTC's actions in this case was its direct lobbying against this proposal. The *New York Times* took note, calling it one of the Council's "infrequent forays into the Washington lobbying scene."[1]

This represented a tremendous mind shift of the Council and its role in foreign trade. Rather than serving as a provider of information or operating in reaction to events, the NFTC now sought to shape American foreign economic policy proactively. During the 1980 presidential campaign, for example, the NFTC sent a memo to both political parties arguing that the federal government had taken too many steps in the past to restrict exports, when what was really needed was a comprehensive policy to increase exports and make trade more nondiscriminatory. The same year, the NFTC held its annual convention in Washington, DC, as a way to attract government support and interest. Except for a brief foray to St. Louis in the late 1940s, this was the first time in more than 40 years that the Council had not held the convention at the Waldorf-Astoria in New York City.[2]

THE WHITE HOUSE

WASHINGTON

October 10, 1979

As the theme of the Sixty-Sixth National Foreign Trade Convention correctly implies, American foreign trade and foreign trade policy are at a critical turning point.

With the advice and support of your Council, we have achieved remarkable success over the past year. The Tokyo Round of multilateral trade negotiations concluded with a virtually new charter to shape international commerce in the decade ahead. The Tokyo Round Agreements, if made to work, will mean that we can continue to move toward freer trade under new rules which are fairer for all.

Also with the advice and support of your Council, we proposed, and the Congress enacted by overwhelming vote margins, the Trade Agreements Act of 1979 to enforce these accords. That Act is one of the most important and far-reaching pieces of trade legislation in this nation's history.

Just last month I submitted to the Congress a comprehensive Executive Branch reorganization plan to streamline our government's efforts to help realize the benefits of the trade agreements and implementing law.

We must continue to work together to make America more competitive in an expanding, healthy world market. Our jobs, our economic growth and vital benefits to our consumers all depend on reaching that objective.

With this in mind, I ask for your sustained support for the objectives we share. I wish you a most stimulating and productive session.

Jimmy Carter

Much of the impetus for this proactive focus came from the member companies of the NFTC who wanted a more forceful advocate for free trade issues in Washington. Many long-term member companies felt that maintaining the Council's headquarters in New York left the organization hamstrung as trade policy was developed in Washington. In response to these growing comments, at the end of 1980, the NFTC began discussing the establishment of a Washington office. A presence in the nation's capital would allow the Council to speak directly to legislators and their staffs, meet with executive agencies, attend Congressional hearings, and engage in direct lobbying.[3]

The move proceeded slowly. The Board deliberated for years on relocating the entire organization to Washington or just parts of it. In the mid-1980s, the Board finally decided to relocate some trade and investment personnel to Washington. However, they also opted not to move the entire organization. Some Council members still relied upon the NFTC to provide educational information about human resources issues that necessitated a close relationship with members' New York offices. After sending several key personnel to Washington and hiring a trade specialist from Citigroup to help staff the office, by 1986 the NFTC had a staff in place and was ready to lobby the omnibus trade bill making its way through Congress.[4]

Omnibus Trade and Competiveness Act of 1988

The NFTC's domestic lobbying efforts intensified during the debate over what eventually became the Omnibus Trade and Competiveness Act of 1988. The Council spelled out policy recommendations for inclusion in the bill. These included enhanced access of United States industry to foreign markets, maximum flexibility for the president in GATT negotiations, increased protection for intellectual property, and repeal of the "windfall profits" tax that it argued would reduce incentives for American companies to explore for oil exports. The NFTC also lobbied to keep certain items out of the bill: automatic remedies for unfair trade practices that limited the discretion of the President; mandated retaliation against countries found to have engaged in unfair practices; the expansion of unfair trade practices to include the denial of worker rights, financing of trade adjustment assistance through an import surcharge; and required notification of plant closing or relocation.[5]

In the past, the Council had issued similar policy recommendations, but what differed now was the sheer amount of time Council staff and members invested actively lobbying Congress. Council staff shaped the trade bill by proposing specific language for the legislation, and thereby succeeded in including many items high on the NFTC agenda, such as presidential fast-track ability, protection of process patents, reduction in licensing burdens in some shipping, more export financing, reduction in the windfall profits tax on oil companies,

October 29, 1981

I am pleased to extend greetings to the officers and members of the National Foreign Trade Council and delegates to the 68th National Foreign Trade Convention.

As one of the largest and most vigorous trade associations in the world, the National Foreign Trade Council has been a major force in educating American business and the American public to the crucial role of trade in this nation's economic growth.

Open markets at home and abroad are vital to a healthy United States economy. Our government is determined to reduce self-imposed export disincentives, uphold U.S. trade laws and international agreements, and reduce government interference in the free flow of trade and investment among nations.

You who are taking part in this 1981 National Foreign Trade Convention represent virtually all viewpoints in the trade community. I am confident your deliberations will make an important contribution to solving problems hampering our nation's position in trade.

In the world of international commerce, business and government must work closely together. I thank you for your effort and wish you success.

Ronald Reagan

adoption of a uniform customs classification system, and ending export controls on items readily available elsewhere in world markets.

The Council also beat back proposed amendments that would have mandated reductions in bilateral trade deficits and that would have discouraged capital inflows by requiring extensive disclosures from foreign investors in the United States. In the end, President Ronald Reagan vetoed the bill because it included plant closing provisions. The NFTC responded by lobbying for the legislation without the plant-closing provision, even though the bill contained some other provisions it opposed, such as requirements for impose import quotas under certain circumstances and a voluntary restraint on steel imports. Congress eventually passed the stand-alone trade bill with overwhelming bipartisan support. The Council's lobbying investment had tangibly paid off.[6]

International Tax Policy, continued

Around this time, the NFTC was also closely tracking tax legislation that threatened or complicated American businesses trading overseas through overregulation. It continued to push for the elimination of double taxation, arguing that the primary right to tax income earned abroad rested with the host country. As a result, it opposed the erosion of the foreign tax credit and the attempts of individual states to tax income earned outside the United States. It instead worked to reduce tax costs for American companies having international operations and advocated competitive tax policies. But despite the Council's efforts, the Tax Reform Act of 1986 restricted the foreign tax credit and accelerated the taxation of foreign source income. The NFTC would fight for the next several years to reinstate the foreign tax credit.[7]

Another age-old tax issue was the one of double taxation, which the NFTC combatted by pushing for tax treaties between nations. These bilateral treaties set out how various countries would collect foreign-source income by multinationals and their subsidiaries. In the absence of multilateral trade agreements, the NFTC sought to implement as many of these treaties as possible. In 1990, for example, members of the NFTC's tax committee met with federal tax officials to encourage a tax treaty between the United States and Brazil. Two years later, the

NFTC aggressively pushed for a tax treaty with Mexico, a top priority for member companies. The NFTC helped to resolve two main issues preventing the treaty's passage: Mexico's asset tax and the withholding tax on dividends paid by units in one nation to parent companies in the other. The NFTC's role in finding solutions to these problems made it a prominent player in the completion of the United States-Mexico treaty.[8]

Managed Trade

Opposition to the plant closing provisions in the 1988 Omnibus Trade Act highlighted the Council's resistance to "managed trade" of any kind, whether through regulations in trade bills, protectionist legislation, tax policy, or sanctions. The NFTC argued that non-managed trade had led to the greatest expansion of world trade, from $61 billion in 1950 to $3 trillion by 1989. Further, managed trade ignored the basic reality of globalization, while at the same time creating scarcities, increasing costs, and turning energy policy in the wrong direction.[9]

Efforts by foreign governments to manage trade also worried the NFTC. With a significant amount of trade conducted with European nations, and the growing integration of the European economic zone, European governmental trade interventions affected NFTC members with interests in Europe. In the early 1980s, the European Economic Community began to cause concerns among Council members. One proposal would have required EEC subsidiaries of multinational corporations to prepare consolidated corporate accounts. This evolved into the Vredeling Directive, which forced parent multinational companies, whether inside or outside Europe, to disclose sensitive information periodically to their workers, such as their financial position, employment plans, and new products. The NFTC, along with the U.S. Chamber of Commerce, opposed this proposed policy as extremely costly and producing a distorted picture of corporate operations. The NFTC sent a 10-member delegation to the EEC committee in Brussels in July 1981 to oppose this and other proposed directives. There, they met with members of the EEC Commission and the European parliament.[10]

Multilateral Market Access

To counter these and other protectionist impulses, the NFTC worked to open up international trade further. To this end, it pushed for multilateral trade agreements as active supporters of the GATT negotiations. As the Uruguay Round neared conclusion, the NFTC rallied the business community, dispensing crucial information and leading support for passage of its implementing legislation by encouraging its member companies to exert their influence with members of Congress.

The NFTC also sought to modify GATT from a system relying on the granting of most favored nation status to one based on mutual market access, which would create a longer-lasting system of reciprocity in goods and services. To this end, it opposed changes to US trade laws that would hinder foreign subsidiaries' operations, and it held conferences explaining the economic impact of the agreement.[11]

The Council also sought to include more countries under multilateral agreements, particularly China. The NFTC actively supported most favored nation (MFN) treatment of China, co-chairing a business coalition on China, lobbying the Hill for passage of MFN status, and bringing together business and Chinese government officials. This proved difficult after the 1989 events in

Tiananmen Square, as members of Congress wanted to grant China MFN status only if it met certain behavioral goals with respect to human rights, and progressed toward the nonproliferation of nuclear weapons. The NFTC claimed victory when President George Bush vetoed the China MFN bill that included these types of provisions in 1992. President Bill Clinton initially took a tougher stance on China, only renewing China MFN with conditions on nonproliferation of nuclear weapons and human rights issues. The NFTC responded in an increasingly direct fashion by focusing on the large number of new members in the House of Representatives. This lobbying effort paid off in 1994 when Clinton delinked China MFN and human rights.[12]

NAFTA

To U.S. companies, the biggest multilateral prize at this time was the North American Free Trade Agreement (NAFTA). Earlier, the NFTC pushed for bilateral tax treaties with both Canada and Mexico that would open up trade. As the details of a more comprehensive continental agreement emerged and came together, the NFTC led lobbying efforts for the bill against fierce opposition both in the US and in Canada. Along with expanding the GATT agreements and securing MFN status for China, passage of NAFTA proved a major lobbying victory for the NFTC and its like-minded business associations.[13]

The Move to Washington, continued

By the middle of the decade, the hybrid approach to keeping the Council's personnel partially in both New York and Washington did not have the impact on the trade debate that many desired. In the fall of 1987, membership secretary Alex Toschi reported that much of the Council membership was still ambivalent about the future of the organization because of its ineffectual presence in Washington. Mainstays of the NFTC, such as Exxon, reported that they did not plan on renewing their membership, citing the Council's continued presence in New York as a reason.

Around the same time, Chrysler departed as well. While corporate troubles had forced Chrysler to withdraw from practically all boards and associations, its representative on the Council complained that the NFTC had been slow to respond on some important issues, such as the targeting of markets by foreign corporations and a failure to address the difficulties in getting American products shelf space in foreign countries. Also, at the time, Chrysler was inclined toward automotive industry protectionism as a means of survival, and it did not see the NFTC, with its underlying free trade philosophy, as particularly helpful in this regard. Other companies followed Exxon and Chrysler in the 1980s, and the NFTC faced a membership crisis. In 1988 alone, 77 companies resigned. This significant decline in membership led to lean years for the Council. The NFTC drew down its reserves, reduced staff, and implemented cost controls.[14]

Merger...or Not?

The NFTC's interest in playing a greater role influencing policies governing international trade, commerce, and investment between America and its major trading partners was evident in its aborted efforts to merge with the United States Council for International Business.[15] In early 1986, the chairmen of the NFTC and USCIB commissioned a joint study on the functioning and effectiveness of the two organizations. This study followed informal discussions with member companies of both organizations and with the concerns they had over the effectiveness of the business community's response to severe international competitive pressures, increasing trade tensions, dangerous tendencies toward protectionism, and other challenges. Advocates hoped the merged organization would more effectively advocate for export expansion, growth of U.S investment abroad, and an open international trading system. The NFTC's actions in Washington and the USCIB's links and interactions with international organizations made the proposed merger advantageous.[16]

The study, by staff of both organizations, reached conclusions supporting the proposed merger. First, the magnitude and complexity of competitiveness issues required extraordinary measures by the business community. Only a group effort could assure an equitable and open system for American trade and investment. Next, the existing organizations available to the business community were inadequate to achieve either business consensus, to address key competitiveness issues, or to advocate on behalf of those issues to Congress or the executive branch. Finally, the complementary strengths of the NFTC and USCIB could provide the organizational and leadership base needed by the business community and act as the primary spokesman in issues of international trade. A merger also would allow greater cost-effectiveness, something necessary in the wake of reduced revenues in both organizations. The USCIB, like the NFTC, faced a corporate world full of mergers and acquisitions, which had reduced the number of available sponsors and members.[17]

With NFTC members registering an overwhelming number of proxy votes approving the merger, everything seemed to be moving toward combining the two organizations; but the NFTC Board of Directors voted against it in November 1986. In doing so, the Board followed the negative recommendation of the implementation committee overseeing the merger negotiations. The committee doubted budget projections that had claimed the merger would not reduce funding. Too many member companies overlapped in membership, meaning that these corporations would cut their dues resulting in major staff reductions and fewer service offerings in a combined organization. The NFTC and USCIB also represented different constituencies, and therefore had somewhat different priorities.[18] As the talks continued, the NFTC began to believe that the proposed organization would not be an equal partnership, and the NFTC's issues would be lost in the shuffle. When the Board finally voted 14 to 6 against the merger, its explanation highlighted financial difficulties as the primary reason for its decision. In a letter to members, the NFTC said this failed proposal would not prevent the NFTC from becoming the leader in advocating for American companies trading abroad. It planned to increase its efforts in Washington, focusing on trade expansion legislation and equitable tax treatment for companies operating abroad.[19]

**Frank Kittredge, NFTC
President 1988-2000**

The Move to Washington, continued

The aborted merger, combined with the increasing financial and membership difficulties, led the NFTC to speed up the move to Washington. Board members had made it clear that a strong Washington presence was the key to the future of the Council. Directors instituted a program to establish the organization as the leading association in Washington on all areas of trade. This would mean that the NFTC headquarters –its president– should operate out of Washington to make the organization as visible as possible to policymakers. This necessitated a search for a new president, as Richard Roberts did not want to relocate from New York.

To succeed Roberts, the board chose Frank Kittredge. Kittredge had spent more than 35 years in GE's international business, most recently as its vice president of international sales development. With a leadership structure in place, the Council next moved to halt the membership decline and even broaden membership. Council Vice President J. Daniel O'Flaherty began to develop a member relations program in the Washington office. This effort to educate non-members on the vital work of the NFTC worked in tandem with an effort by Board members to use their personal contacts to encourage new companies to join. The Chairman encouraged all Board members to come to meetings with a list of potential members for the Council. The Board then divided this list and lobbied these companies to join. [20]

The Sanctions Niche

The precarious position of the NFTC and the now-crowded Washington marketplace of trade associations made it necessary for the NFTC to find a niche for itself in the national political conversation. It did so with great effectiveness over the contentious issue of economic sanctions. The NFTC had long opposed government actions that restricted American trade or created a situation that would encourage retaliatory trade action. Although modern-era sanctions began with the Cuba Embargo in 1960, the use of sanctions exploded in the 1980s and 1990s, when governments and other institutions commenced using sanctions as a primary tool of foreign policy. In response, the NFTC in the mid-1980s formed an economic sanctions working group. In 1989, this group put together a plan to respond to the renewal of the Export Administration Act which authorized the US President to control exports to promote foreign policy objectives, comply with international obligations, or deter and punish terrorism. The NFTC sanctions working group pushed for more favorable language in this renewal, working to develop alternative mechanisms to sanctions.[21]

The Council underwrote a study by Georgetown University Professor Gary Hufbauer documenting the cost of sanctions to the American economy. Hufbauer began his study with a historical overview. Since 1914, the American gov-

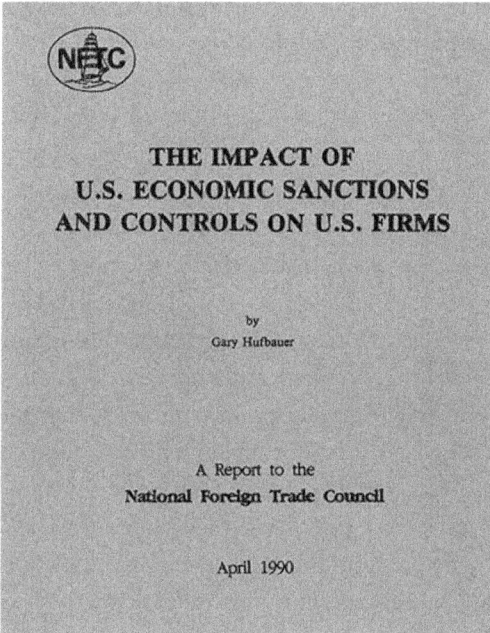

(NFTC logo)

**THE IMPACT OF
U.S. ECONOMIC SANCTIONS
AND CONTROLS ON U.S. FIRMS**

by
Gary Hufbauer

A Report to the
National Foreign Trade Council

April 1990

ernment had imposed sanctions 74 times. Of these attempts, 39 had worked, but Hufbauer said those seeming successes came with a few caveats: most were not unilateral, and very few had worked recently. The most obvious reason for the declining effectiveness of unilateral sanctions was the decline of the American economy relative to the rest of the world. Further, the objectives of sanctions had changed over the course of 75 years. They worked best when they sought to destabilize undesirable governments. But the federal government now deployed sanctions for other purposes: improving human rights, deterring nuclear proliferation, and combating terrorism. Using sanctions in these ways rarely worked and was counterproductive. [22]

Hufbauer also noted that economic sanctions cost American business nearly $7 billion of revenue annually. American firms could no longer engage in commercial activities with certain target countries and were unable to bid on particular foreign projects. Unilateral foreign policy sanctions also disproportionately hurt certain American businesses. For some sanctions regimes, the entire burden fell on just a few companies because they were in narrowly defined, specialized industries. These companies – exporters with petrochemical, manufacturing, or other industrial specializations – made up a significant portion of the NFTC's member base. Hufbauer found that European countries used foreign policy sanctions much less frequently, and business that would have gone to American firms went to European ones instead. Once this market share was lost, it could decades to regain.[23]

Hufbauer suggested automatic sunset provisions that would force Congress to re-enact sanctions legislation every few years. Also, he advocated that Congress should have to seek advisory opinions from the International Trade Commission before enacting sanctions in order to guarantee that the United States does not violate any trade agreements. Finally, Hufbauer noted that sanctions should be based in common sense. If the targeted country can already acquire non-military, non-technical goods from other countries, then there is no reason American businesses should be left at a disadvantage.[24] Hufbauer concluded that because of the significant loss of business and dubious efficacy of sanctions, the federal government should re-examine their use to maximize effectiveness with the least cost to the American economy.

Divestment and the U.S.-South Africa Business Council

The conclusions of the Hufbauer study and its policy recommendations guided the Council's early actions concerning sanctions. The NFTC's first major sanctions battle came over South

Africa. In the late 1970s and early 1980s the anti-apartheid movement increased in numbers and power. Anti-apartheid activists encouraged institutional investors to divest from all American businesses that did business in South Africa or had not adopted the Sullivan Principles. On behalf of its members, the NFTC paid increasing attention to these developments. It circulated materials about the principles and tracked their adoption by companies. As this protest movement gained strength, the NFTC sent a letter to members of Congress in September 1983 urging them to oppose legislation that would require companies to adopt the Sullivan Principles.[25] While the NFTC publicly affirmed that it deplored apartheid, it maintained that sanctions were not an effective means to end it.

Divestment furor reached a fevered pitch after the South African government violently put down domestic resistance to apartheid. Numerous colleges and universities, 26 states, 22 counties, and more than 90 cities sold off South African-related investments or refused to do business with companies operating in South Africa took economic action against companies doing business in South Africa. Some governments gave preference in bidding on goods and services to companies that did not do business in South Africa. As the divestment movement gained momentum, the NFTC discussed the possibility of bringing suit against these state and local statutes that penalized companies for having ties to South Africa. The board of directors went so far as to instruct Council staff to see if the organization would have standing in such a case.[26]

As the NFTC considered how to respond to this spate of state and local divestment efforts, Congress passed a Comprehensive Anti-Apartheid Act in 1986. The act banned new U.S. investment in South Africa, sales to the police and military, new bank loans, and the import of a variety of agricultural goods, textiles, foodstuffs, and raw materials. Because of the adverse impact these sanctions would have on its members, the Council organized a coalition to stop Congress from implementing these new sanctions. The NFTC-led coalition hired a PR firm to lead a campaign that would show that most American companies doing business in South African didn't support the policy of apartheid and that their presence in South Africa worked to undermine apartheid.[27]

In early 1988, W.R. Grace, a founding Council member, reported to the Board on the negative economic effects sanctions had on its business. Since it was an election year, the Board pushed the Council to take on a greater leadership role in convincing the public that American businesses were not pro-apartheid and to turn back the increasing number of sanctions. This included trying to repeal the Rangel Amendment, a 1988 provision that denied foreign tax credits to American companies' income earned from businesses in South Africa.[28]

As leaders of the business coalition opposing sanctions, NFTC staff members organized a fact-finding mission to South Africa with Council member companies. Upon return, the staff reported that it had visited the office and facilities of member companies in-country, examined social responsibility projects, and met with academics and black union leaders. This visit allowed Council staff to share the insight that demographic trends, particularly the significant rise of the black population, would severely test the ability of the ruling group to retain its stranglehold on power.[29]

Council staff predictions proved correct with the ending of apartheid in the early 1990s. These moves to end this discriminatory policy resulted in the federal government lifting sanctions. With national sanctions no longer preventing American businesses from operating in South Africa, the Council next moved on two fronts. As the chair of a business coalition seeking to overturn South African sanctions, the NFTC sought to repeal remaining state and local sanctions by convening a national conference on investment in South Africa. Vice President Dan O'Flaherty published articles on the business situation and opportunities in South Africa in the prestigious journal *Foreign Affairs*.

The Council also took on a new, different and more permanent role. After being approached by a number of businesses, the NFTC founded the U.S.-South Africa Business Council, its first foray into the realm of bi-lateral business councils. This subsidiary unit of the NFTC focused its activity on repealing state and local sanctions and opposing proposed corporate codes of conduct, such as one in Massachusetts that required American companies to consider social questions before investing overseas.[30]

The Council had significant successes as leader of the U.S.-South Africa Business Council. It sustained efforts to end sanctions, resulting in about three quarters of the 190 sanctions being repealed by the middle of the 1990s. As the number of sanctions decreased, the NFTC and South Africa council moved more towards an advisory role. They published a bi-weekly newsletter filled with information about their efforts, news clippings about the political and economic situation in South Africa, and specialized materials about economic opportunities in South Africa, while continuing to advocate for open markets in South Africa with more flexible and open labor policies.[31]

This move from seeking to lift sanctions to encouraging new investment as part of an official bilateral business commission culminated in an appearance of Nelson Mandela before the NFTC's annual World Trade Dinner. On his first visit to the United Sates, Mandela spoke before the NFTC at the Waldorf-Astoria, the site of so many prior NFTC conventions. His appearance gave both Mandela and member companies a place to connect and promote business

Nelson Mandela with NFTC Chairman Patrick Ward
(Caltex Petroleum) at the 1994 World Trade Dinner

opportunities. As evidence of their pivotal role in opening the South African market, staff members of the NFTC traveled to South Africa with the U.S. Vice President and Commerce Secretary to establish the Gore-Mbeki Binational Commission, headed by Vice President Gore and Deputy President Mbeki.[32]

Coalition for U.S.-Vietnam Trade

The successes in South Africa led the Council to take the lead in pursuit of permanent normal trade relations (PNTR) with Vietnam. As far back as the 1980', in letters to then-Secretary of State James Baker, the NFTC urged the federal government to accelerate the resumption of full trade relations. Since the fall of Saigon, the American government had enforced a trade embargo with Vietnam, renewed annually since 1975. Beginning in the early 1990's American businesses sought to end the embargo because Vietnam had now grown into of one of the 20 largest foreign markets. The Council argued that failure to improve relations would leave Americans shut out of a major market for sales of heavy equipment and participation in the development of the nation's oil fields. Delaying resolution of the issue were the families of unaccounted servicemen who wanted the fates of missing Americans resolved through POW/MIA searches before the American government normalized trade.[33]

Members of the NFTC saw normalization of trade relations with Vietnam as one of the most important Council initiatives. Just as in South Africa, the Council sent a fact-finding mission of staff and member company personnel to Vietnam to examine the economic situation, improve ties, and seek ways through which American firms could convince the federal government to overturn the embargo. And, again, just as with South Africa, it organized business opposition to the trade embargo, founding the Coalition for U.S.-Vietnam Trade. The Coalition spoke on behalf of numerous private companies, used business connections to lobby government officials, and provided a centralized attack on the

Vietnam trade embargo. The Council and Coalition targeted their efforts on the renewal of the Trading With the Enemy Act. It hoped it could convince Congress to allow the Act to lapse, effectively eliminating the ban on trade with Vietnam.[34]

With increased pressure on the federal government and the economic assistance from non-governmental organizations (NGOs), Vietnam began assisting in the location of MIAs from the Vietnam War. This combination approach of carrot-and-stick led President Clinton to lift the trade embargo on Vietnam in February 1994, a significant political victory for the NFTC and its allies. The NFTC now turned its energy toward publicizing the commercial opportunities now available in Vietnam. It held conferences and seminars on doing business in Vietnam, bringing together business and government officials on both sides to talk business for the first time in a generation. This lobbying and educational work came to fruition with the signing of a Bilateral Investment Treaty (BIT) in 2001.[35]

Launch of USA*Engage

Successful NFTC activities in South Africa and Vietnam pointed to deeper worries among Council members. By the middle of the 1990s, American companies became more outspoken against the unintended consequences of unilateral sanctions. Rather than affecting change as the designers of sanctions intended, these policies were rarely effective and hurt American businesses. Allied Signal and Caterpillar, both members of the NFTC, spoke out forcefully in the press. Caterpillar went so far as to circulate a map among legislators showing where American sanctions had created obstacles for their business efforts. These companies and others echoed some of the arguments from the Hufbauer report: trade sanctions were ineffective and becoming an increasingly frequent tool for the American government. Further, in a large, complex and fluid global marketplace, trade sanctions could not be enforced in any meaningful way.[36]

These deepening worries led the NFTC to take formal steps to oppose unilateral sanctions. At a board meeting in June 1996, Bill Lane, an executive with Caterpillar and a member of the Council's trade and investment committee, presented the results of a survey of Council members. Lane reported that many members had serious concerns over the increasing use of unilateral economic sanctions. Members believed the business community was losing the policy argument over the efficacy and necessity of these kinds of actions. The Board and member companies thought the NFTC, as an umbrella organization and respected voice of the foreign trade community, could play a pivotal role because of the delicacy in opposing sanctions against nations such as Cuba, Iran, Libya, Colombia, Nigeria, Myanmar, China, Russia, South Africa, or

Vietnam. In response, the NFTC solicited bids to launch a campaign that would discredit unilateral sanctions by showing their impotence, how they hurt American workers, and in fact rewarded foreign companies by allowing them to take business opportunities forbidden to American firms. [37]

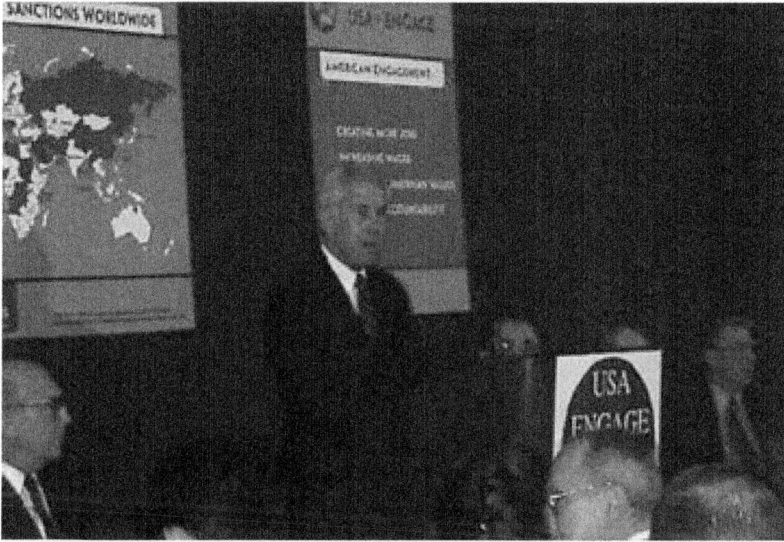

Indiana Senator Dick Lugar speaking to USA*Engage in the late 1990s.

Within a few months, the NFTC hired the Wexler Group and the law firm of Hogan & Hartson to assist with the sanctions project, named USA*Engage. The project quickly acquired significant support from Council members and other businesses, claiming more than 600 member companies. Focusing its efforts on regional and local newspapers, the USA*Engage campaign stimulated more than 200 editorials on sanctions, most favoring the NFTC's position. USA*Engage reprinted and disseminated these editorials questioning the use of unilateral sanctions.

USA*Engage focused on the passage of the Hamilton-Lugar bill as a tool of sanctions reform. This legislation promised to protect overseas contracts signed at the time sanctions were imposed and would require sanctions to automatically expire after two years unless specifically reauthorized. USA*Engage urged its member companies to contact their local legislators to support the Hamilton-Lugar legislation. Their lobbying efforts persuaded a number of senators and members of the House of Representatives to sign up as co-sponsors, but the bill failed to pass Congress.

Another particularly effective technique for USA*Engage was the issuance of Congressional report cards. It graded each member of Congress based on their opposition to sanctions and other restrictive trade measures. Items included in the report card included religious persecution sanctions, normalization of trade relations with China, Jackson-Vanik waiver for Vietnam, state and local sanctions, fast track negotiating authority, and repeal of Section 907 banning direct American aid to the Azerbaijani Government.[38]

Supreme Court Victory: The *Crosby* Case

In the latter part of 1997, USA*Engage raised the possibility of a constitutional challenge to state and local sanctions. It had considered a lawsuit before in the case of South Africa, but the Council had ultimately decided against it. The opportunity arose again in the mid- to late-1990s when dozens of state and local governments passed selective-purchasing laws, targeting nations such as Indonesia, Nigeria, Switzerland, and Cuba.

The most numerous of these locally-passed sanctions laws targeted the military junta in Myanmar. The cities of New York, Los Angeles, and Philadelphia, joined Massachusetts and Vermont in imposing laws prohibiting doing business with firms active there. With USA*Engage, the Council spent several months searching for a law it thought it could challenge on constitutional grounds. It decided to focus on a legal challenge to the Massachusetts law requiring the state to refrain from making purchases from companies that did business in Myanmar.[39]

The law was effective, in that it forced Apple to pull out of Myanmar if it wanted to keep its contracts with Massachusetts. Eventually, 34 members of the NFTC ended up on the state's restricted-purchase list. The NFTC filed suit against Stephen Crosby, the Massachusetts Secretary of Administration and Finance, arguing that these types of laws were unconstitutional because they infringed upon the federal government's exclusive control of American foreign policy. Circuit and federal judges agreed with the NFTC, setting up Supreme Court arguments in the fall of 1999.[40]

To finance *Crosby vs. the National Foreign Trade Council,* the NFTC collected surcharges from member companies in addition to their regular dues. To add heft and gravitas to the challenge, the Board made the strategic decision to have the Council serve as the public face of this constitutional challenge, rather than USA*Engage, because the Council was the pre-eminent representative of American companies trading abroad. The case garnered a significant amount of public attention for the NFTC. The 15 states of the European Union filed an *amicus* brief asking the judges to find the policy unconstitutional. The case also became a lightning rod for anti-globalization sentiment.

Groups focused on human rights picketed the Supreme Court in support of the Massachusetts bill, carrying signs such as "Boston Tea Party 2000" and "EU out of Boston Harbor."

In a major victory for the NFTC, the Supreme Court unanimously overturned the Massachusetts law in June 2000. The justices ruled the state's purchasing law violated the Supremacy Clause of the Constitution, which gives Congress the power to pre-empt state laws. The Massachusetts law also eliminated the President's flexibility and discretion in conducting US foreign policy, and that the divergence between state law and federal sanctions compromised the ability of the President to be the sole voice of American foreign policy. Therefore, the Massachusetts law was judged unconstitutional.

The Ex-Im Bank

While its campaign against sanctions took up an increasing amount of the Council's time, it still remained active in several longstanding efforts, particularly related to Congressional reauthorization of Export-Import Bank. Many NFTC members relied upon the Ex-Im bank for financing and insuring foreign purchases of United States goods for customers wary of credit risk. The Council saw a greater economic good in the Export-Import Bank. They argued that the bank increased exports and jobs, returned money to the US treasury, reduced inflation, and made export activities possible when traditional banks dared not tread.[41]

Because of the export-oriented nature of the NFTC, it had a long, close association with the Export-Import Bank. During the Depression, the NFTC had been an influential backer in the creation of the bank, so that there would be a body to provide long-term financing for exports. Throughout the next five decades, members of the Council supported its extension and expansion. Various Export-Import Bank officials spoke before the NFTC convention, such as Warren Pierson, president of the Bank, in 1945. One consistent refrain from the NFTC was a concern that the Bank would become a political football. During once such battle for reauthorization in 1963, the Council issued a statement warning that each day the bank was neutered and not allowed to extend financing meant the loss of significant sales volume.[42]

The politicization of the Bank climaxed in the 1980s with debates over cuts to the federal budget. In his first budget, President Reagan sought to sharply reduce the budget of the Export-Import Bank. For him, it was another federal agency that needed to borrow on the federal debt market at a time when government credit demands were squeezing borrowers. As a consequence, the Bank could not offer financing at competitive terms. The situation grew so dire that the Bank temporarily suspended lending in 1981. To address these systemic problems, the NFTC lobbied Congress to create a mechanism for off-budget authorizations. This pool of funds would provide flexibility, and it would be used if the United States could not reach international agreements on competitive export financing. [43]

For much of the 1980s the NFTC's efforts on behalf of the Export-Import Bank were unsuccessful. With a drastically reduced budget, its

The foreign-trade strategy proposed in FORTUNE amounts to unilateral disarmament just when protectionism is on the rise worldwide.

A Difference of Opinion

Let's Hear It for the Export-Import Bank   by Richard W. Roberts

At a time of great concern about the ability of the U.S. to compete effectively in world markets, it was odd to see FORTUNE march off in the other direction by publishing an article suggesting that the Export-Import Bank be abolished ("Export-Import Follies," August 25). The author, Steven E. Plaut, an assistant professor of economics at Oberlin College, advances arguments that seem strangely out of touch with the brutally competitive real world in which American exporters are trying to survive and prosper. Plaut acknowledges that other countries subsidize exports but thinks we should welcome these cheap imports as a gift from foolish foreigners. If the trade balance worsens, "a small depreciation of the dollar" will put things right.

Playing with fire

In the real world, however, a cheaper dollar is anything but a panacea. It is true that as our currency loses value, our exports become less expensive, but a cheaper dollar also raises the cost of imports and so adds to the inflationary pressures in the U.S. economy.

Moreover, the dollar is the world's principal reserve currency, and a trade strategy that encourages its depreciation amounts to playing with fire. Depreciations have a way of getting out of hand, as the dollar's sinking spells in recent years have demonstrated. Last year the flight from the dollar assumed panic proportions, and the Treasury and the Federal Reserve were obliged to take tough countermeasures. The Fed forced interest rates up sharply, and the Treasury orchestrated a worldwide campaign to support the dollar.

Plaut describes concerns about the trade balance as "a holdover from mercantilist days." He refers here to the 18th-century doctrine that nations should try to achieve a large surplus in trade, even by predatory behavior in international markets. Unfortunately, when it comes to export financing, mercantilism is alive and well in many countries, including such industrial powerhouses as Japan and France. This doctrine, which the National Foreign Trade Council joins FORTUNE in deploring, promises to be a dominant theme in international economics during the 1980s. The U.S. government and the American business community support the position that export-credit agencies around the world should operate at commercial interest rates and terms—without government subsidies. However, until an effective international agreement is reached among the major trading nations to eliminate such predatory financing, these "gift horses," in the form of subsidized exports by our trading competitors, should be examined with the caution that history and common sense suggest. In the long run, such unfair trade practices are harmful to consumers. Once the dominant foreign producer—subsidized by his government and immune to U.S. antitrust laws—has wiped out his U.S.

competition, he is able to raise prices. In the end, the effects on domestic employment and economic stability are extremely adverse. The foreign-trade strategy proposed in FORTUNE amounts to unilateral disarmament just when protectionism is on the rise worldwide.

Perhaps that wouldn't matter if governments didn't intervene in foreign-exchange markets, if exchange rates were isolated from the effects of capital flows and were immediately responsive to changing patterns of trade—and if, in addition, multibillion-dollar export sales were made in the sort of international bazaar that Plaut imagines to exist. In this imaginary arena, the U.S. is still the dominant trader and can afford to say, "Here it is, that's our price, go get the money and we will sell."

The Third World wants to buy

In the real world, adequate financing is a key element in most export transactions and it is absolutely vital in the case of capital goods, the bulwark of our manufactured exports. A recent report of the Congressional Research Service describes the competitive situation this way: "The growing commercial rivalry among the developed countries and the increasing similarities in the price, quality, and availability of their goods has meant that, in many cases, government financing arrangements have become a determining factor. In the capital-goods sector, and 'big ticket' items in particular, it now often appears that contracts may go to the exporter who is able to arrange the most attractive financing for his sale." This is nowhere so true as in the case of sales to the developing countries, with their immense needs for

Richard Roberts is president of the National Foreign Trade Council, supported by 650 U.S. companies.

Photograph by Marianne Barcellona

resources continued to shrink until the Bank had to suspend lending once again in 1989. As in 1981, this development provoked a critical outcry from the trade community, especially when the trade deficit stood at $130 billion. The Bank continued to guarantee loans made by commercial banks, but it eliminated direct loans, which had long been one of its core products. [44]

By the end of the 20th century, however, the Bank's fortunes began to turn. The NFTC, now ensconced in Washington, participated in a vigorous lobbying campaign to restore funding. Along with the National Association of Manufacturers (NAM) and the Coalition for Employment Through Exports (CEE), it planned major trade conferences on export financing to seek ways to overcome the billions of dollars lost due to the lack of competitive official financing. Council members testified before Congress concerning the Bank's diminishing resources and the need for government financing for American exports. Besides increased financing, staff members continued to push for improved guarantees on commercial bank loans and the use of direct credit authority to make up the difference between commercial lending rates and official export credits.[45]

Foreign Corrupt Practices Act

Politicization of trade issues also provoked anxiety among the NFTC in regards to the Foreign Corrupt Practices Act (FCPA). Passed in 1977 during the height of the conflict about the size and function of multinational corporations, the FCPA prevented multinationals from making payments or gifts to intermediaries or agents of foreign governments to obtain or retain business. Almost immediately upon its passage, the NFTC complained about the interpretation of the FCPA by the Securities and Exchange Commission and the Department of Justice. The Council thought that overly rigid enforcement discouraged American companies from pursuing legitimate business opportunities around the world. Further, it argued that the act was overly complex, vague, and subject to varying interpretations. In an essay in the *New York Times*, Frank Roberts, the chairman of the NFTC subcommittee on the FCPA, laid out the Council's position. It advocated for amendments to eliminate ambiguities relating to agents or intermediaries and the scope of exceptions for expediting (grease) payments. The NFTC also proposed that the Justice Department be given sole enforcement power over the act, clearing up jurisdictional questions that created uncertainty in the business community. Finally, it pushed for amendments to eliminate the criminal provisions of the bill.[46] Senior Vice President William Baldwin Jr. led the Council's FCPA efforts.

Growth of Existing Programs: Tax and International HR

The Council remained a repository of vital information for American companies trading abroad, but the kind of information changed. With a globalized world, companies no longer needed basic economic information about foreign countries or even the steps needed to open overseas branches. What they needed was far more specialized knowledge. The NFTC filled this knowledge gap in the areas of taxation and human resources. Both were some of the most requested areas of information of member companies. Filling these roles provided a unique service to member companies and comprised part of the Council's outreach strategy to attract new members.

As international taxation became more and more complicated, the NFTC held numerous seminars and conferences to keep member and non-member companies abreast of current tax law, as well as proposed changes and their ramifications. It began to hold an annual tax retreat for tax lawyers and governmental officials in Scottsdale, Arizona. These retreats helped to explain how businesses could best comply with complicated tax laws. The NFTC's retreats and seminars also kept member companies and attendees current on global tax policy, cross-border acquisitions, and business performance metrics. The Council also began holding a fall tax conference in Washington DC, designed to attract key government speakers based in the nation's capital. [47]

In the realm of international HR, the Council had long kept data on expatriate compensation, occasionally compiling surveys of employee allowances. The U.S. government and many businesses relied on a Council publication called "Maximum Travel Per Diem Allowances for Foreign Areas" to set their own employees' overseas allowances.

More importantly, however, the Council expanded its emphasis to providing advice in all areas of international human relations, including immigration and competitiveness. [48]

This specialized international HR knowledge operated on two levels. Smaller companies entering the global marketplace needed practical assistance concerning basic issues of operating a business overseas, where the Council had significant experience. On the other hand, larger companies had greater concerns about keeping overseas personnel costs down in order to remain competitive. The NFTC worked with these differing constituencies as appropriate. For smaller companies, the Council provided surveys, manuals, reports, and seminars on labor and economic conditions, such as a 1989 seminar on these kinds of issues in Taiwan and the Philippines. For larger firms, it provided cost-savings ideas for expatriate staff. The Council also brought in executives from multinationals in Japan and Europe to share ideas about how they handled their staffs. [49] Foreign firms also wanted information from the NFTC about personnel policies in the United States. In 1990 Mitsui asked the Council to sponsor a multi-day seminar in Japan for Japanese firms who wanted to know more about American personnel practices. Similarly, the International Human Resources Committee met in China in February 1996 to discuss sourcing, retention, and housing.[50]

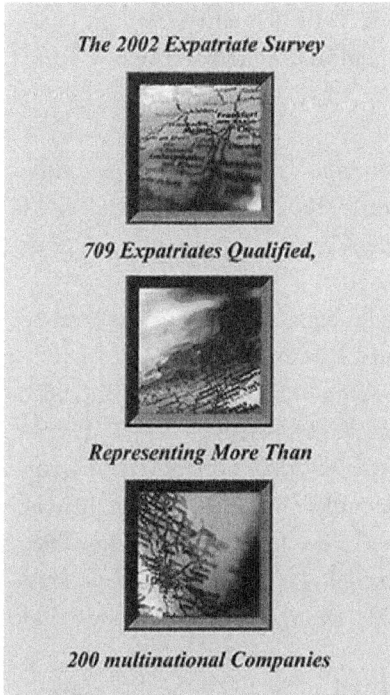

The 2002 Expatriate Survey

709 Expatriates Qualified,

Representing More Than

200 multinational Companies

These expanded forays into questions of international human resources brought a significant amount of positive attention to the NFTC, which formalized its International HR division in New York, hiring William Sheridan in 1993. The increased activity centered on sharing best practices and cost-saving measures for large companies, while still retaining the Council's institutional knowledge on questions of expatriate compensation, as evidenced by regular articles in *The Journal of International Compensation and Benefits*. It also partnered with Towers Perrin in a well-regarded study of international compensation that surveyed 200 benchmark companies. By 1998, more than 325 member companies participated in some aspect of the Council's human resources functions, and many non-member companies attended these conferences as well.[51]

As the 20th Century drew to a close, the NFTC was re-energized with a new orientation towards lobbying, leadership on niche issues relating to sanctions, international taxation, and human relations, and chairmanship of bilateral business councils. Together, these shifts allowed the NFTC to weather the storms of the 1980s and 1990's, and indeed to make significant progress. And while these new practice areas represented a major shift in the tactics of the Council, each was still an extension of the organization's long-standing commitment to an open, expansionist system of rules-based international trade. While the organization still worried about its finances, expansion in these areas vividly demonstrated how the NFTC would remain relevant in the now-crowded marketplace of trade associations and lobbying groups.

Chapter Endnotes

[1] "Washington Watch," *New York Times,* June 21, 1982.

[2] "NFTC Board Meetings, 1980" (National Foreign Trade Council, 1980), National Foreign Trade Council Records, Box 7; "NFTC Board Meetings, 1981" (National Foreign Trade Council, 1981), National Foreign Trade Council Records, Box 7.

[3] "NFTC Board Meetings, 1980."

[4] "NFTC Board Meetings, 1986" (National Foreign Trade Council, September 1986), National Foreign Trade Council Records, Box 23, Folder 10; "NFTC Board Meetings, 1987" (National Foreign Trade Council, April 1987), National Foreign Trade Council Records, Box 23, Folder 16.

[5] "NFTC Board Meetings, 1987" (National Foreign Trade Council, October 1987), National Foreign Trade Council Records, Box 24, Folder 1.

[6] "NFTC Board Meetings, 1987" (National Foreign Trade Council, April 1987), National Foreign Trade Council Records, Box 23, Folder 16; "National Foreign Trade Council Objectives and Current Projects" (National Foreign Trade Council, 1988), National Foreign Trade Council Records, Box 24, Folder 2; "NFTC Board Meetings, 1988" (National Foreign Trade Council, March 1988), National Foreign Trade Council Records, Box 24, Folder 3; "Omnibus Trade Bill" (National Foreign Trade Council, May 31, 1988), National Foreign Trade Council Records, Box 24, Folder 4.

[7] "NFTC Board Meetings, 1988" (National Foreign Trade Council, December 1988), National Foreign Trade Council Records, Box 24, Folder 5.

[8] "NFTC Board Meetings, 1990" (National Foreign Trade Council, October 1990), unprocessed; "A Special Summary and Forecast Of Federal and State Tax Developments," *Wall Street Journal* (New York, May 13, 1992).

[9] "NFTC Board Meetings, 1990" (National Foreign Trade Council, May 1990), unprocessed.

[10] "NFTC Board Meetings, 1980" (National Foreign Trade Council, 1980), National Foreign Trade Council Records, Box 7; "NFTC Board Meetings, 1981" (National Foreign Trade Council, 1981), National Foreign Trade Council Records, Box 7; "Workers Have a Right to Know More," *New York Times,* October 3, 1982.

[11] "NFTC Board Meetings, 1982" (National Foreign Trade Council, 1982), National Foreign Trade Council Records, Box 7.

[12] "NFTC Board Meetings, 1990" (National Foreign Trade Council, May 1990), unprocessed; "Display Ad 27 — No Title," *Wall Street Journal,* May 29, 1990;

"NFTC Board Meetings, 1991" (National Foreign Trade Council, October 1991), unprocessed; "NFTC Board Meetings, 1990"; "NFTC Board Meetings, 1992" (National Foreign Trade Council, October 1992), unprocessed; "NFTC Board Meetings, 1993" (National Foreign Trade Council, June 1993), unprocessed; "NFTC Board Meetings, 1993" (National Foreign Trade Council, October 1993), unprocessed.

[13] "NFTC Board Meetings, 1991"; "NFTC Board Meetings, 1992" (National Foreign Trade Council, January 1992), unprocessed; "NFTC Board Meetings, 1992"; "NFTC Board Meetings, 1993" (National Foreign Trade Council, January 1993), unprocessed; "NFTC Board Meetings, 1993"; "NFTC Board Meetings, 1993"; "NFTC Board Meetings, 1994" (National Foreign Trade Council, March 1994), unprocessed; "NFTC Board Meetings, 1995" (National Foreign Trade Council, February 1995), unprocessed.

[14] "NFTC Board Meetings, 1987" (National Foreign Trade Council, October 1987), National Foreign Trade Council Records, Box 24, Folder 1; "NFTC Board Meetings, 1989" (National Foreign Trade Council, February 1989), unprocessed; "NFTC Board Meetings, 1989" (National Foreign Trade Council, June 1989), unprocessed.

[15] United States Council for International Business (USCIB) is an independent business advocacy group originally founded in 1945 to promote free trade and help represent U.S. business in the, then new, United Nations.

[16] "NFTC Board Meetings, 1986."

[17] Ibid.

[18] The USCIB at the time was very oriented toward Europe and its interests, and its policies were largely driven more by service-oriented industries, such as banks and law firms, than by the manufacturing sector.

[19] "NFTC Board Meetings, 1986" (National Foreign Trade Council, June 1986), National Foreign Trade Council Records, Box 23, Folder 9; "NFTC Board Meetings, 1986" (National Foreign Trade Council, November 21, 1986), National Foreign Trade Council Records, Box 23, Folder 14.

[20] "NFTC Board Meetings, 1988" (National Foreign Trade Council, March 1988), National Foreign Trade Council Records, Box 24, Folder 3; "NFTC Board Meetings, 1988" (National Foreign Trade Council, June 1988), National Foreign Trade Council Records, Box 24, Folder 4; "NFTC Board Meetings, 1988" (National Foreign Trade Council, December 1988), National Foreign Trade Council Records, Box 24, Folder 5.

[21] "NFTC Board Meetings, 1989."

[22] Gary Hufbauer, *The Impact of U.S. Economic Sanctions and Controls on U.S. Firms* (National Foreign Trade Council, April 1990).

[23] Ibid.

[24] Ibid.

[25] "NFTC Board Meetings, 1983" (National Foreign Trade Council, 1983), National Foreign Trade Council Records, Box 23, Folder 2.

[26] "NFTC Board Meetings, 1987."

[27] "Business Group Lobbies to Stop Congress From Imposing Sanctions on South Africa," *Wall Street Journal*, April 28, 1988.

[28] "NFTC Board Meetings, 1989" (National Foreign Trade Council, October 1989), unprocessed; "NFTC Board Meetings, 1990" (National Foreign Trade Council, May 1990), unprocessed; "NFTC Board Meetings, 1990" (National Foreign Trade Council, October 1990), unprocessed.

[29] "NFTC Board Meetings, 1989."

[30] "NFTC Board Meetings, 1993" (National Foreign Trade Council, January 1993), unprocessed; "NFTC Board Meetings, 1993" (National Foreign Trade Council, June 1993), unprocessed; "NFTC Board Meetings, 1993" (National Foreign Trade Council, October 1993), unprocessed.

[31] "NFTC Board Meetings, 1994" (National Foreign Trade Council, March 1994), unprocessed; "NFTC Board Meetings, 1995" (National Foreign Trade Council, June 1995), unprocessed.

[32] "Mandela Begins U.S. Visit With a Side Trip to Harlem: He Is Greeted by Big Crowds Near Church," *New York Times,* October 3, 1994; "NFTC Board Meetings, 1997" (National Foreign Trade Council, February 1997), unprocessed.

[33] "U.S.-Vietnam Ties Remain Held Back By the MIA Issue," *Wall Street Journal,* December 2, 1991.

[34] "NFTC Board Meetings, 1993"; "NFTC Board Meetings, 1993"; "NFTC Board Meetings, 1994."

[35] "NFTC Board Meetings, 1995"; "NFTC Board Meetings, 1998" (National Foreign Trade Council (October 1998), unprocessed.

[36] "Who's Punishing Whom?: Trade Bans Are Boomerangs, U.S. Companies Say Who Punishes Whom in Trade Bans?," *New York Times,* September 11, 1996.

[37] "NFTC Board Meetings, 1996" (National Foreign Trade Council, June 1996), unprocessed.

[38] "NFTC Board Meetings, 1998."

[39] "The Foreign Policy Issue: Justices Overturn a State Law on Myanmar," *New York Times,* (New York, June 20, 2000.

[40] "NFTC Board Meetings, 1997"; "NFTC Board Meetings, 1997" (National Foreign Trade Council, October 1997), unprocessed; "Limiting a State's Sphere of Influence: Judge Rejects Law on Myanmar as Foreign Policy Infringement," *New York Times,* November 15, 1998.

[41] "NFTC Board Meetings, 1980" (National Foreign Trade Council, 1980), National Foreign Trade Council Records, Box 7.

42 "Final Declaration of the Twenty-First National Foreign Trade Convention," November 1934, National Foreign Trade Council Records, Box 78, Folder 26; "Address of the Chairman and Annual Reports of the National Foreign Trade Council," March 1935, National Foreign Trade Council Records, Box 24, Folder 12; "Final Declaration of the Twenty-Second National Foreign Trade Convention," November 1935, National Foreign Trade Council Records, Box 78, Folder 37; "Preliminary Program, 32nd National Foreign Trade Convention," November 1945, National Foreign Trade Council Records, Box 78, Folder 37; F.W. Magalhaes, "Report on the Twenty-Seventh National Foreign Trade Convention," August 9, 1940, National Foreign Trade Council Records, Box 78, Folder 32; "Trade Group Worried," *New York Times*, July 15, 1963.

43 "NFTC Board Meetings, 1980"; "Ex-Im Bank Vs. Budget Cutters," *New York Times*, February 13, 1981.

44 "New Loans Suspended By Agency: Ex-Im Bank's Move Is Result of Cuts in Final Reagan Budget," *New York Times*, January 9, 1989.

45 "NFTC Board Meetings, 1989" (National Foreign Trade Council, June 1989), Unprocessed.

46 "NFTC Board Meetings, 1980"; "NFTC Board Meetings, 1981" (National Foreign Trade Council, 1981), National Foreign Trade Council Records, Box 7; "A Chance to Correct The Core Problem," *New York Times*, March 20, 1983; "Omnibus Trade Bill" (National Foreign Trade Council, Inc., May 31, 1988), National Foreign Trade Council Records, Box 24, Folder 4; "NFTC Board Meetings, 1993" (National Foreign Trade Council, October 1993), unprocessed.

47 "NFTC Board Meetings, 1996" (National Foreign Trade Council, Inc., February 1996), unprocessed; ibid.

48 "NFTC Board Meetings, 1968" (National Foreign Trade Council, 1968), National Foreign Trade Council Records, Box 5; "NFTC Board Meetings, 1990" (National Foreign Trade Council, October 1990), unprocessed; "What U.S. Pays for Trips," *New York Times*, December 4, 1988.

49 "NFTC Board Meetings, 2000" (National Foreign Trade Council, October 2000), unprocessed; "NFTC Board Meetings, 1990" (National Foreign Trade Council, May 1990), unprocessed; "NFTC Board Meetings, 1989" (National Foreign Trade Council, June 1989), unprocessed.

50 "NFTC Board Meetings, 1990"; "NFTC Board Meetings, 1996."

51 "NFTC Board Meetings, 1993" (National Foreign Trade Council, June 1993), unprocessed; "NFTC Board Meetings, 1993" (National Foreign Trade Council, October 1993), unprocessed; "NFTC Board Meetings, 1998" (National Foreign Trade Council, October 1998), unprocessed.

CHAPTER SIX

Into the Twenty-First Century

By 2000, the NFTC was the premier business-led advocate for open, rules-based trade. The organization had all of the programs and policies in place to complete its transition to a largely lobbying organization. The Council was comfortably in place in Washington. It had had several high-profile legislative successes, and had found niche issues to exert influence. While its purpose was set, the NFTC underwent another series of personnel changes. Frank Kittredge and Alex Toschi retired in 2000 and 2001, respectively, taking with them more than 50 years of collective organizational experience. In addition, the Council continued to suffer from financial difficulties that dated back to the 1980s.

By naming William Reinsch President in 2001, the NFTC board demonstrated its commitment to the organization's new priorities. Past presidents of the Council had all come from the New York corporate world. But the bulk of Reinsch's career had been as a Washington insider, as Undersecretary of Commerce in the Clinton Administration and earlier as a legislative aide to Senators John Heinz and Jay Rockefeller. Choosing a President with extensive political experience and good relations on both sides of the aisle demonstrated that the Council wanted to firmly position the NFTC in the center of the Washington political world.

NFTC President Bill Reinsch, 2001-

Its updated mission statement symbolized this transition. While remaining faithful to long-standing Council initiatives, the NFTC wanted to advance global commerce through public policies that fostered open international trade and investment. Promotion of such legislation occurred through the mobilization of expertise and information on key issues, including taxes, trade finance, economic sanctions, and international human resources. The Council sought to influence public debate through interaction with policy makers and opinion leaders. With the success of the sanctions issue, and the continued relevance of the Council in trade policy, international taxation, and international human resources, the NFTC had a clear path forward into the next century. [1]

USA*Engage

By 2001, USA*Engage was the highest-profile endeavor of the NFTC. Government and business interests recognized the Council and USA*Engage as the lead organizations on sanctions. Acquiring this expertise also gave the Council a vital niche among trade associations. Very few businesses or trade organizations wanted to get involved in the politically fraught issue. With the defeat of the Hamilton-Lugar Sanctions Reform bill, which would have changed the procedure for imposing of unilateral US sanctions, and the successes in the Myanmar case, the NFTC and USA*Engage faced the question of what to do next with this significant and very successful endeavor. Members still believed that the danger of unilateral sanctions would continue and that governments would continue to erect barriers to trade.[2] In addition, the NFTC has maintained its longstanding effort to persuade the Congress to repeal legislation that effectively forced the government to remove a trademark that had been lawfully issued to a Cuban entity, thus exposing the hundreds of U.S. trademarks registered in Cuba to the possibility of retaliation.

There was no shortage of sanctions issues for USA*Engage and the Council to work on. Government sanctions remained for places like Cuba and Iran, where the federal government often worked to tighten these policies. New sanctions also were enacted against countries such as Somalia. State and local governments continued to impose divestment measures against nations with poor human rights records, such as Sudan. Supporters of sanctions increasingly utilized a new strategy: the obscure Alien Tort Claims Act, where foreign citizens could take American companies to court for violating the law of nations or of treaties with the United States. Through the filing of amicus briefs challenging the constitutionality of state and local laws that infringed upon the federal government's exclusive jurisdiction in foreign policy matters, USA Engage and the NFTC spent a significant amount of time opposing the use of this 18th Century law for 21st Century foreign policy.[3] Vice President Richard Sawaya, Executive Director of USA*Engage, does exceptional work on these issues.

Cuba consumed much of the debate over sanctions. For years, the NFTC had called for an end to the Cuba embargo. For the Council, the embargo was an antiquated and ineffective provision that cost trade and jobs while European and Canadian firms dominated a market just miles from U.S. shores. During the Bush Administration, the NFTC lobbied the House of Representatives to lift the travel ban for Cuban-Americans, increasing humanitarian assistance, and eliminating prohibitions on private financing of agricultural and medical sales. With the Bush Administration instead committed to tightening sanctions, these efforts did not succeed. After 2009, the Obama Administration liberalized portions of the embargo. The NFTC praised these moves and used it as an opportunity to push for repeal of the entire embargo. To move the debate toward this goal, the Council participated in an exploratory mission to Cuba organized by the Washington, DC-based Center for International Policy. Like the trips to South Africa and Vietnam in years past, this trip allowed the NFTC to learn about the local political and economic situation, develop possible future business contacts, and demonstrate the business community's resolve to ultimately end the embargo. [4]

USA*Engage continued to build on the success of the *Crosby v NFTC* Supreme Court decision. It wrote governors and state legislators to warn them about continuing to undertake divestment actions or sanctions by themselves in the wake of the *Crosby* decision. These warnings included opposition to requirements that pension fund managers divest shares of companies with business ties to Sudan. These warnings generally went unheeded. States continued to pass divestment bills, prompting the NFTC to sue the state of Illinois to challenge successfully the constitutionality of its Sudan divestment bill, forcing Illinois to rewrite its sanctions law. [5]

USA*Engage also led business efforts to combat the growing use of the Alien Tort Statute. Plaintiffs used the provision to hold American multinationals responsible for human-rights abuses by foreign countries. The ATS was part of the Judiciary Act of 1789 and was intended to deal with the prosecution of international pirates in American courts. Now, lawyers were attempting to use this 200 year-old legislation to make it more difficult for multinationals to do business with repressive regimes. The first salvo on this new front began in 2003 when the energy company Unocal was sued for aiding and abetting human-rights abuses that Myanmar inflicted on villagers during the building of a natural-gas pipeline. Council president Bill Reinsch commented in the *New York Times* that these acts could be disastrous for global trade with their combination of sympathetic plaintiffs, trial lawyers, and anti-globalization activists. While no ATS cases had come to trial, Reinsch noted that companies already had rethought investment decisions and pulled back from projects in countries accused of human-rights abuses. [6]

The Myanmar-Unocal case came to the Supreme Course with another case, *Sosa v. Alvarez*. USA*Engage submitted an *amicus* brief, arguing that they both subverted the federal government's foreign policy, arguing that these lawsuits hurt the economy and business, resulting in lost American investment overseas. It also made a public case against the ATS through press interviews and speeches, such as that at the Rutgers University Law School in 2004. In addition, USA*Engage staff petitioned the State Department to discourage the use of Alien Tort cases because of their detrimental effect on American foreign policy. [7]

The MEFTA Coalition

Under USTR Robert Zoellick, armed with presidential Trade Promotion Authority, the number of free trade agreements (FTAs) under negotiation exploded in the first decade of the new century. The NFTC began to play a major role in sanctions and trade questions relating to the nations of the Middle East. Under the aegis of the Middle East Free Trade Area (MEFTA) business coalition, organized and led by the NFTC, the Council sought to open up trade throughout the Middle East. This meant opposing unilateral sanctions on Iraq and Iran and other measures designed to change national policies in certain Middle Eastern nations. These efforts also meant finding ways for American companies to increase their business opportunities in Middle East countries, as well as full engagement in the business coalitions for the Jordan, Morocco, Bahrain, and UAE free trade negotiations.

USTR Robert Zoellick speaking at the MEFTA Coalition Kickoff Event, 2004

In the cases of Free Trade Agreements with Morocco, Bahrain and Oman, the NFTC established business coalitions to lobby and coordinate business efforts to pass these agreements. Lobbying for these FTAs included events to draw attention to their value. For instance, the kickoff event supporting the U.S.-Morocco FTA featured United States Trade Representative Bob Zoellick, Secretary of Commerce Don Evans, and Moroccan Foreign Minister or Minister for Foreign Affairs and Cooperation Taib Fassi-Fihri. Discussions about these FTAs came to include joint strategic planning with FTA partner governments and their lobbying teams, as well as discussions around implementation and ways to publicize the new market opportunities to U.S. businesses. [8]

With the conclusion of the first phase of the Iraq War in 2009, the Council and USA*Engage convened meetings with member companies, American governmental officials, and Iraqis about rules changes and business opportunities for U.S. firms in the reconstruction of the country. The NFTC and USA*Engage also worked with countries in the Middle East to convince them to liberalize their economies. In the case of Saudi Arabia, this meant promoting its accession to the WTO, while advising the Kingdom of the necessary internal changes that accession required. NFTC efforts with the MEFTA Coalition proved extremely successful, growing to encompass more than 125 supporting organizations and associations, and is still an active coalition today, led by Vice President Chuck Dittrich.[9]

Business Immigration

In the wake of the terrorist attacks of September 11, 2001, one of the most difficult issues for American businesses was new restrictions on the movement of people across American borders. In response, USA*Engage and the NFTC worked to become the leading advocates for changes in visa requirements that would allow normal international commercial travel, through 'trusted traveler' programs and other innovations that would not compromise security. Mobility of persons and data become a chief policy goal. They believed the State Department should have increased flexibility to expedite visas. USA*Engage showed the detrimental effects of these restrictive rules on America companies' ability to perform routine business transactions through meetings with the executive branch and through industry meetings for member companies to discuss their experience with delays. Surveys of member companies allowed USA*Engage to quantify the loss of business resulting from visa delays. USA*Engage also feared the loss of American prestige, focusing attention on the growing problem of poor treatment of business visitors at points of entry.[10] Legitimate commercial travelers should not be stymied by extraordinary security measures.

Trade Policy Leadership

The main leadership role for the NFTC came, naturally, in the arena of trade policy, just as envisioned when it shifted its headquarters to Washington DC. The NFTC's long-established and well-regarded Trade and Investment Committee still determined NFTC trade initiatives and led all related activities for the Council. Subcommittees worked on areas of concern both new and well-known to the Council. A Tariff Working Group sought to find ways to reduce tariffs in multilateral trade agreements, and a globalization group made a positive case for liberalizing world trade.

In 2002, the NFTC played a major role in a broad campaign for passage of renewed trade promotion authority (TPA). This authority, which would provide the President with multi-year negotiating power, was essential to any serious trade negotiations and thereby finalizing and implementing multilateral trade agreements, since it required the Senate, with the possibility of

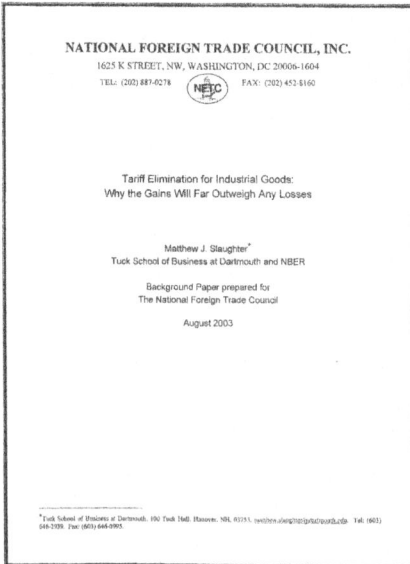

amendments, to approve or disapprove trade deals that the Executive Branch had negotiated.

Since TPA lapsed in 2006, the NFTC has been consistent in its call for renewal. The political moment seemed right in 2013-14 when the progress of both the Trans-Pacific Partnership (TPP) and Trans-Atlantic Trade and Investment Partnership (TTIP) talks had the Obama administration considering requesting TPA renewal. The NFTC was at the forefront of the issue, releasing in April of that year the first draft TPA bill for consideration by the House Ways and Means Committee and Senate Finance Committee. A number of its provisions and suggestions were adopted in the version of the bill that was formally introduced several months later.

The NFTC bolstered its leadership credentials in Washington yet again with the 2011 election of Alan Wm. Wolff as its Chairman. Ambassador Wolff, Senior Counsel at the firm of McKenna Long and Aldridge LLP, served as Deputy USTR for Trade Negotiations, leading U.S. trade policy formulation during the GATT Tokyo Round (1977-1979). He also served as General Counsel of the USTR from 1974-1977. A distinguished statesman well respected in Washington trade policy circles, Amb. Wolff provides *gravitas* and authority for the NFTC when he engages on any trade policy issue, and has been deeply involved in TPP and other global trade policy issues issues on behalf of the Council.

Export Control Reform

Given the experience of Council President Bill Reinsch as former Undersecretary for the Bureau of Industry and Security, it is only natural that the Council has become a leading voice for the international business community on the complex export control reform (ECR) efforts of the Obama administration. The NFTC serves as the secretariat for The Coalition for Security and Competitiveness, which closely monitors the reform process and provides a forum for its members to discuss the various proposals within ECR among themselves and with the Administration officials responsible for implementing them. The NFTC has consistently supported the reform effort. In its view, the old export control process was needlessly complicated, burdensome on U.S. business, confusing or unclear about some key details, and has not kept up with current changes in technology or marketplace availability. In the long term the results of the ECR effort will be advantageous to NFTC members, although short term transition issues may cause some difficulties. In particular, simplification of the process and moving items off the controlled list are outcomes the NFTC wholeheartedly supports.

The WTO Project

WORLD TRADE ORGANIZATION

To encourage the WTO to begin a new multilateral round of negotiations, the NFTC launched "The WTO Project" in March of 2001, under the leadership of Procter and Gamble. Later that year, the WTO launched the Doha Round of WTO negotiations (or Doha Development Agenda) with the vocal support of the NFTC. For this round, the Council sent delegations to the WTO in Geneva to show business support for the trade talks, encouraged an ambitious agenda to eliminate all industrial tariffs and open up new markets for American companies, and focus greater attention from multilateral bodies like the WTO and World Bank on trade capacity building in developing countries. As the Doha negotiations stalled, the NFTC's WTO Project issued white papers and other communications in attempt to break the logjam. The Council also worked to galvanize international support through major panel sessions at the annual WTO public forum.[11]

When the WTO reached an agreement at Bali in late 2013 on Trade Facilitation, the NFTC was there and actively engaged. The Council quickly assembled comments from its members, then published and circulated the first detailed 'post-Bali Agenda' for consideration by the WTO, earning the public thanks of WTO Director General Roberto Azevêdo on his next visit to Washington for its support and leadership on WTO matters.

As to services, the NFTC has been and remains a staunch supporter of the Trade in Services Agreement (TISA) talks, on behalf of its member companies who provide services worldwide. In conjunction with other business associations like the U.S. Coalition of Service Industries, the NFTC supports a high standard agreement to allow U.S. services to compete in global markets on a level playing field.

Bilateral FTAs

With little progress occurring at the Doha talks, the NFTC encouraged the U.S. government as it turned its attention to the negotiation of multiple bilateral FTAs. The NFTC supported these agreements over a dozen countries, partnering with wide business coalitions in support of their Congressional passage. As one example, Vice President Anne Alonzo founded The Hispanic Alliance for Free Trade in support of the DR-CAFTA agreements. In the early 2010s, the most important of these agreements were Colombia, Panama, and South Korea. The NFTC played a leading role in the fight for Congressional passage of these FTAs. More than five years following the completion of negotiations, Congress finally approved the remaining three agreements as a package in 2011. The NFTC lobbied new House GOP members and the White House in support of all three deals. Coordinating their efforts with leading companies, and in alliance with the U.S. Chamber of Commerce and other business associations, they were able to overcome long-standing opposition from labor unions and others.[12] Like all FTA's, they will create well-paying U.S. jobs as exports grow, and strong commercial relationships tend to develop stable allies.

Russia PNTR

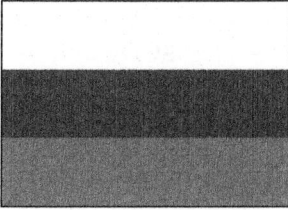

The Council consistently pushed for normalization of trade relations; in the decade of 2010, this meant Russia. The NFTC believed that bringing this market into the rules-based world trading system would create major opportunities for its members and other U.S. businesses. By 2012, Russian membership in the WTO had already been approved. But for U.S. companies to take advantage, extending permanent normal trade relations (PNTR) to Russia meant exempting it from the Jackson-Vanik Amendment, the law that denied normal relations with the Soviet Union until it liberalized its immigration policy for Jewish citizens. Inability to extend PNTR meant that American companies would not have the same opportunities as the other 153 WTO members, and that Russia could issue retaliatory legislation. The NFTC argued that failure to extend the PNTR would mean the loss of billions of possible dollars in services, agriculture, manufacturing, and high-tech sectors, as companies from other countries would rush into the market. In the summer and fall of 2012, the NFTC lobbied to advance this legislation, but it faced a hurdle in the form of the Magnitsky Rule of Law Accountability Act, which would punish Russian violators of human rights through entry bans or asset freezes. [13] The NFTC and USA*Engage worked very hard, with some success, to rewrite the Magnitsky provisions to make them more administrable. Ultimately Russia PNTR passed the Congress and was signed by President Obama in December 2012 with the Magnitsky Rule attached, allowing U.S. companies to operate on a level playing field in this important growing market.

"Buy America" Provisions

During the financial crisis of 2008, as in the past occurrences of economic contraction, protectionists argued that free trade policies exported jobs overseas. In response, some protectionists called for "Buy America" provisions or legislation, often at the state or local level. Consistent too with those past episodes, the NFTC lobbied Congress, presidential candidates, state legislators and even state attorneys general to rebut these efforts. As part of this effort, it created a legislative guide to explain the illegality of these provisions, and issued a major study about the global economy and supply chain management. This piece explored the dramatic shift from an international economy based on exports and imports to a system of global corporate supply chains. To make these supply chains feasible and to compete internationally, American companies relied heavily on open borders in order to trade and move goods quickly. The data showed the trading patterns of companies present in more than 100 countries, demonstrating just how far the global trade situation had evolved in just over a generation from the emergence of the first multinationals to the predominance of complicated global supply chains. [14] The NFTC closely tracks "Buy America" provisions and discourage state legislatures from enacting them because they intefere with the federal government's role as the leader of U.S. foreign policy.

21st Century Trade Issues

The dawn of the 21st Century coincided with the rise of new set of trade problems. The digital age fostered connections consumers and producers worldwide in unprecedented ways, forcing questions about the role and rules surrounding data as a primary trade mode. Elsewhere, questions were being asked publicly and privately worldwide about the role of trade in causing, if not preventing, global climate change. And as the U.S. economy faltered in the 2008 financial crisis, innovation and competitiveness policies became nearly synonymous with efforts to create a sustainable post-industrial economy for the U.S. The NFTC embraced these policy challenges with enthusiasm and ingenuity.

Digital Trade

NFTC and its Foundation began early in the new century to explore new issues surrounding global innovation and doing business in a globally-connected, technology-driven world. Led by several member companies, the Council spearheaded business community efforts to develop new trade rules for the global digital marketplace. In 2011, in conjunction with a coalition of like-minded business associations, the Council issued a document outlining the principles of promoting global flows of digital information, calling for new protections for companies and individuals to send and receive digital data. At the same time, the Council focused on the challenges that the explosion of digital information posed to companies doing business across borders in the 21st Century, such as differing privacy rules, intellectual property rights (IPR) rules and protections, and localization regulations, especially in the context of new threats such as digital theft of trade secrets.

Trade and Climate Change

At the same time, the NFTC and its member companies realized that trade policy could be used to address the global issue of climate change; in fact, as early as 1974 the Council had *ad hoc* working groups on the impact of trade on the environment. In 2009, NFTC launched its Trade and Climate Change working group, chaired by United Technologies, to address key policy issues relevant to global trade in clean technologies. Through this working group, NFTC emphasizes the role of IPR in the development and deployment of clean technologies and of lowering tariffs on environmentally-friendly products and services, participating in UN climate policy meetings and supporting the development of commitments under the Asia Pacific Economic Cooperation (APEC) forum to lower tariffs on green goods. As a result of this groundwork, the NFTC was named as a co-chair (along with the NAM and US CIB) of the Business Coalition for Green Trade at the Environmental Goods Agreement (EGA) talks at the WTO in 2014 with the goal of tariff-free trade in environmental goods, so that consumers and governments worldwide can take immediate advantage of environmentally friendly technologies and products.

The Global Innovation Forum

Global **Innovation** Forum

As part of the focus on innovation and national competitiveness, in January 2009 the NFTC Foundation established the Global Innovation Forum, whose goal is to convene start-ups, small businesses, development professionals, academics and other stakeholders to discuss how public policy can solve critical global challenges and contribute to shared prosperity. The Forum highlights the growing role of small businesses and entrepreneurs in the global marketplace. Beginning in 2010 with a grant from the GE Foundation, the NFTC Foundation held a series of dialogues involving small businesses located in U.S. These discussions, held over several years in innovation and manufacturing hubs such as Chicago, Cincinnati, Pittsburgh, Denver, Austin and Research Triangle Park in North Carolina, brought small business CEOs and NFTC member companies together in a unique dialogue with educators and public policy officials to highlight the opportunities and challenges of accessing global markets. The discussions highlighted areas where new policies could help businesses improve their ability to operate globally, from improving the global protection of intellectual property rights to altering U.S. immigration and visa policies. In October 2012, NFTC member company eBay led a public discussion about the growing role of small businesses in international commerce, and the positive role that an open global digital marketplace plays in economic development. Vice President for Global Trade Issues Jake Colvin is the Executive Director of the Global Innovation Forum.

International Tax Policy for the 21st Century

One of the major tax initiatives in the early 2000s was an outline of a simplified tax system that would better reflect the state of the modern economy. For instance, the NFTC worked toward an electronic commerce tax system that did

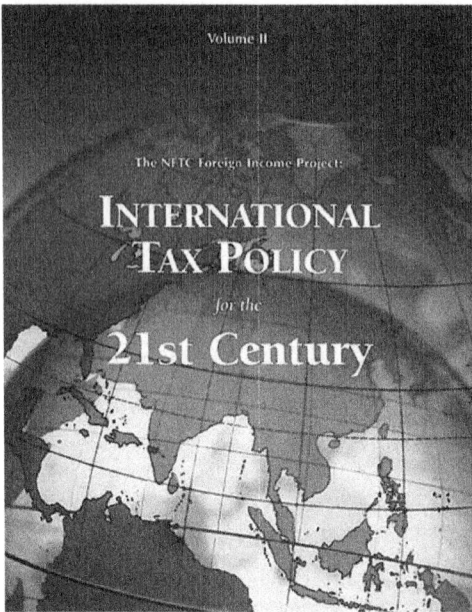

not discriminate between electronic and traditional commerce, provided geographic neutrality, and promoted the growth of global electronic commerce. The NFTC lobbied Congress to support its passage. [15]

To further this and other tax goals, the NFTC formed four tax-oriented working groups: legislative, tax treaty, regulatory, and non-U.S. issues. The Legislative Group works to coordinate Congressional efforts for the NFTC international tax bill. The Regulatory group tracks and seeks to influence regulatory changes within the administration, typically the Treasury Department and the IRS. The Tax Treaty Group provides input to the Treasury Department about which countries the business community believes should be priorities for bilateral tax agreements, and gives formal comments and critical feedback on negotiations as they progress. The Non-U.S. Group works to find areas for the Council to track, analyze and influence issues in foreign countries concerning proposed tax legislation. The NFTC communicates to foreign governments how proposed legislation might negatively affect American companies or multinationals doing business within their borders. [16]

In 2001, the NFTC laid out a series of innovation and far-reaching tax policy prescriptions in its publication *International Tax Policy for the 21st Century*, among its most popular titles in the past few years. Some of the issues addressed there have become today's thorniest tax issues, such as the Base Erosion/Profit Shifting (BEPS) project of the OECD, and the legislative battle over the investment/tax tactic commonly referred to as inversion. The NFTC continues to call for comprehensive, sensible tax reform to allow businesses to compete in a transparent, predictable tax environment while meeting reasonable government revenue needs. This could save companies millions of dollars in taxes, promoting growth of exports and jobs. The International Tax program at the NFTC has been expertly led over the years by Fred Murray and Judy Scarabello, and today is headed by Vice President for Tax Policy Cathy Schultz.

The Foreign Sales Corporation (FSC) Debate

One of the hottest tax issues the NFTC charged into was the defense of Foreign Sales Corporation (FSC) benefits. The debate over the modification of the program in the early 2000s split the American trade community. The difficulty began when the WTO declared FSCs an illegal trade subsidy. It ruled that they inappropriately provided a huge benefit to multinationals by allowing American companies to reduce their taxes on profits by channeling sales through financial instruments based in low-tax countries. Council members saved hundreds of millions of dollars per year as a result of these programs. The NFTC worked toward a potential solution, but its consensus approach was overshadowed by Congressman Bill Thomas, who wanted to shift the benefits of the FSCs to multinationals with extensive factories or services overseas. This would have burdened smaller companies that had regularly done business overseas for many years. As a result, the proposal divided the membership of the Council based on which members stood to gain the most. With this internal division, the NFTC kept its members informed of the latest developments but could no longer pursue an active advocacy role on the issue. [17]

International HR, continued

In international human resources, the NFTC continued to hold seminars around the nation on benefits, compensation, and other issues of concern for expatriates, as it has for years. The NFTC's International HR program engages executive leaders of corporate global human resources departments to find solutions, understand best practices, and highlight management trends in the increasingly globally mobile workplace. What ties together its human relations endeavors is a commitment to making global talent mobility an integral part of U.S. trade policy. To that end, the Council participated in and promoted the global mobility project, which called for the more efficient processing of business-sponsored work permits and visas. After September 11, it also developed programs that connected human relations policies to the challenges of global terrorism. Global violence affected the physical security of expatriates and their financial assets, interrupted business, raised insurance costs, and affected cross-border trade.[18] Still based in New York City, the International HR program also works closely with the NFTC's tax program and Global Innovation Forum when issues overlap, giving members the benefit of expertise from across the HR and policy spectrums. Vice Presidents Bill Sheridan and Grace O'Rourke lead these efforts for the NFTC.

Transoceanic Plurilateral Agreements

By 2007, it became increasingly evident to the Bush Administration that the Doha Round of WTO negotiations were proving more difficult to realize than previous rounds, given the large number of participating countries and increasingly disparate levels of development. Therefore the U.S. sought to identify opportunities to engage in the Asia Pacific with like-minded nations, and to similarly consolidate its near-continuous dialog with the European Union (EU) while preserving its fundamental commitment to the multilateral process.

In the Pacific, the U.S. identified a small innovative effort of the "P-4" nations of Chile, New Zealand, Singapore and Brunei as an opportunity to pursue a broader Pacific free trade zone. Using this plurilateral effort as a platform, it soon grew to include 12 key markets in the region (Chile, New Zealand, Singapore, Brunei, U.S., Australia, Vietnam, Malaysia, Peru, Mexico, Canada and Japan) by 2013. Now known as the Trans Pacific Partnership (TPP), it is a phased negotiation that combines high ambition with architecture that encourages new entrants. Building on its experience with the MEFTA coalition, the NFTC became heavily engaged from the outset of these talks, and remains an active member of the business coalitions in support of them. The NFTC provides key feedback from its members, and is relied upon by negotiators, business working groups, and even foreign governments for its expertise in many areas. The Council supports an ambitious agreement with high standards, especially in the areas of freedom of cross border data flow, disciplines on state-owned enterprises, and labor and environmental protections.

Across the other ocean, NFTC members account for a large proportion of the Trans-Atlantic economy, so the Council had been deeply involved for years in the economic policy making process on both sides. NFTC and its members provided key input to both parties as the US-EU High Level Working Group neared its deci-

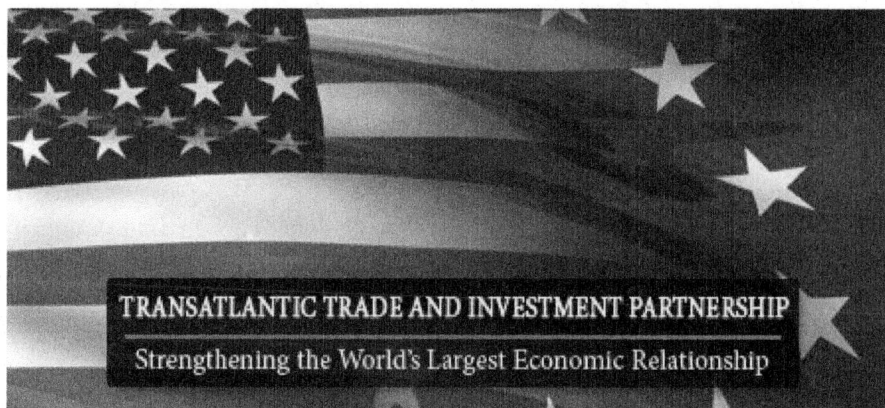

TRANSATLANTIC TRADE AND INVESTMENT PARTNERSHIP

Strengthening the World's Largest Economic Relationship

sion to formally launch the Trans-Atlantic Trade and Investment Partnership (TTIP) in June 2013. Today the NFTC co-chairs 5 separate working groups for the business coalition in support of TTIP: Regulatory, Intellectual Property, Digital Trade, Global Mobility, and Competition (State Owned Enterprises, or SOEs.) As a practical matter, tariff levels between the US and EU are already extremely low due to the shared legacies of open trade philosophy and prior GATT/WTO rounds. The stickiest issues may be in the regulatory and investment chapters of this potential agreement, which could substantially eliminate the remaining barriers in what is already the world's largest trade and investment relationship.

In these dual efforts among nations committed to growth, job creation, and innovation, the NFTC has been engaged from the outset. The Council was involved in the precursor efforts that suggested the strategic shift, the early explorations of modalities and selection of partner nations, and the preservation of each effort's commitment to a strong multilateral approach to a rules-based world trading system. Vice President Chuck Dittrich coordinates the council's TPP and TTIP activities.

The Forward March

Today, as in 1914, the NFTC serves America's global businesses, remaining fully committed to an open, expanding world trading system. With over 200 member companies, the NFTC continues to engage and speak out as the authoritative voice of the American international business community.

For its next one hundred years, the NFTC will have its hands full, remaining actively engaged in handling a packed slate of international business issues such as the WTO, multi- and bi-lateral trade negotiations, regulatory harmonization, trade facilitation, capacity building, preference programs, non-tariff barriers, export credit agencies, export controls, sanctions, competitiveness, innovation, currency and exchange rates, advanced manufacturing, trade in environmental goods, cross-border data-flows, international tax and investment issues, and international human resources and business immigration. It is a widely repeated fact that ninety-five per cent of the world's customers live outside the U.S.A. The NFTC will continue to make it its job to open markets worldwide to U.S. goods, services and investment, within a rules-based framework that maintains a level, transparent, predictable playing field. When these conditions exist, businesses and nations prosper.

The National Foreign Trade Council has undergone a great many changes during its first century. It began as an informal group that brought together American businesses interested in expanding markets abroad for their goods, services and investments. They gathered regularly for meetings and conventions, dealing with periods of expansion, global economic downturns, wars, crises and recovery. It became the pre-eminent source for Americans seeking information about international trade, and began to shape public policy and support international trade agreements on behalf of its members. The NFTC has retained all these functions to become a forceful voice advocating for free, open, rules-based global trade. Despite the many challenges America and the global trading system have faced during its 100 year history, the NFTC has remained steadfast and true to founding Chairman James Farrell's call for American businesses to work together to foster greater prosperity with our trading partners through increased trade, forming a more peaceful world through closer commercial ties.

Chapter Endnotes

1 National Foreign Trade Council, "National Foreign Trade Council 2001 Priorities," 2001, Unprocessed.

2 National Foreign Trade Council, "NFTC Progress and Accomplishments in 2001," 2001, Unprocessed.

3 "NFTC Board Meetings, 2009" (National Foreign Trade Council, October 2009), Unprocessed; "NFTC Board Meetings, 2008" (National Foreign Trade Council, June 2008), Unprocessed; National Foreign Trade Council, "National Foreign Trade Council 2003 Priorities," 2003, Unprocessed; National Foreign Trade Council, "National Foreign Trade Council 2006 Priorities," 2006, Unprocessed; National Foreign Trade Council, "National Foreign Trade Council 2007 Priorities," 2007, Unprocessed; National Foreign Trade Council, "National Foreign Trade Council 2008 Priorities," 2008, Unprocessed; National Foreign Trade Council, "National Foreign Trade Council 2009 Priorities," 2009, Unprocessed; National Foreign Trade Council, "National Foreign Trade Council 2010 Priorities," 2010, Unprocessed; National Foreign Trade Council, "National Foreign Trade Council 2011 Priorities," 2011, Unprocessed; National Foreign Trade Council, "National Foreign Trade Council 2012 Priorities," 2012, Unprocessed.

4 National Foreign Trade Council, "National Foreign Trade Council 2003 Priorities"; National Foreign Trade Council, "National Foreign Trade Council 2004 Priorities," 2004, Unprocessed; National Foreign Trade Council, "National Foreign Trade Council 2009 Priorities"; National Foreign Trade Council, "National Foreign Trade Council 2010 Priorities"; National Foreign Trade Council, "National Foreign Trade Council 2011 Priorities"; "NFTC Board Meetings, 2009" (National Foreign Trade Council, June 2009), Unprocessed; "NFTC Board Meetings, 2010" (National Foreign Trade Council, September 2010), Unprocessed.

5 National Foreign Trade Council, "National Foreign Trade Council 2007 Priorities"; "NFTC Board Meetings, 2007" (National Foreign Trade Council, October 2007), Unprocessed; National Foreign Trade Council, "National Foreign Trade Council 2008 Priorities."

6 Alex Markels, "Showdown for a Tool In Rights Lawsuits," *New York Times* (New York, June 15, 2003); Steve Lohr, "Who's Afraid of China Inc.?" (New York, N.Y., United States, July 24, 2005), sec. Section 3; Steve Lohr, "Advisory Commission Urges Congress to Get Tough on China Trade," *New York Times* (New York, November 9, 2005).

[7] National Foreign Trade Council, "National Foreign Trade Council 2004 Priorities"; National Foreign Trade Council, "National Foreign Trade Council 2005 Priorities."

[8] National Foreign Trade Council, "National Foreign Trade Council 2004 Priorities."

[9] National Foreign Trade Council, "NFTC Progress and Accomplishments in 2002," 2002, Unprocessed; National Foreign Trade Council, "National Foreign Trade Council 2005 Priorities," 2005, Unprocessed; National Foreign Trade Council, "National Foreign Trade Council 2006 Priorities"; National Foreign Trade Council, "National Foreign Trade Council 2007 Priorities"; National Foreign Trade Council, "National Foreign Trade Council 2008 Priorities"; National Foreign Trade Council, "National Foreign Trade Council 2012 Priorities."

[10] "Bill Reinsch" interview by Nathaniel Wiewora, August 9, 2012, Unprocessed; "Dan O'Flaherty"; National Foreign Trade Council, "National Foreign Trade Council 2006 Priorities"; National Foreign Trade Council, "National Foreign Trade Council 2008 Priorities"; National Foreign Trade Council, "National Foreign Trade Council 2012 Priorities."

[11] National Foreign Trade Council, "National Foreign Trade Council 2003 Priorities"; National Foreign Trade Council, "National Foreign Trade Council 2005 Priorities"; National Foreign Trade Council, "National Foreign Trade Council 2008 Priorities"; National Foreign Trade Council, "National Foreign Trade Council 2012 Priorities"; "NFTC Board Meetings, 2011."

[12] "Bill Reinsch"; "NFTC Board Meetings, 2009."

[13] "Bill Reinsch"; "Dan O'Flaherty"; "NFTC Board Meetings, 2012" (National Foreign Trade Council, June 2012), Unprocessed.

[14] "Dan O'Flaherty"; National Foreign Trade Council, "National Foreign Trade Council 2009 Priorities"; National Foreign Trade Council, "National Foreign Trade Council 2010 Priorities."

[15] "Bill Reinsch"; "Dan O'Flaherty"; National Foreign Trade Council, "National Foreign Trade Council 2004 Priorities."

[16] National Foreign Trade Council, "National Foreign Trade Council 2006 Priorities."

[17] "Bill Reinsch"; Edmund L. Andrews, "A Civil War Within a Trade Dispute: Growing Fallout from Retaliatory Tariffs by the European Union.," *New York Times* (New York, 2002), sec. Business Day.

[18] "Bill Reinsch"; "Dan O'Flaherty"; National Foreign Trade Council, "NFTC Progress and Accomplishments in 2002."

APPENDIX A

Chairmen and Presidents

NFTC Chairmen (1914-present)

1914 – 1943	James A. Farrell, President of United States Steel Cooperation
1943 – 1945	Eugene P. Thomas, Vice President of United States Steel Cooperation
1945 – 1947	John Abbink, President of the McGraw-Hill International Corporation
1947 – 1957	Robert F. Loree, Vice President of Morgan Guaranty Trust
1957 – 1962	George W. Wolf, President of United States Steel Cooperation
1962 – 1963	James A. Farrell Jr., President of Farrell Lines
1963 – 1969	E. S. Hoglund, Executive for GM
1969 – 1976	Robert J. Dixson, President of Johnson & Johnson
1976 – 1979	James M. Roche, Chairman and CEO of GM
1979 – 1981	J. Kenneth Jamieson, Chairman and CEO of Exxon
1981 – 1984	William S. Anderson, Chairman of National Cash Register Corp (NCR)
1984 – 1987	Robert Frederick, President and COO of RCA
1987 – 1989	(No Chairman)
1989 – 1991	Charles Hugel, Chairman of Asea Brown Boveri and RJR Nabisco
1991 – 1993	Donald Fites, Chairman and CEO of Caterpillar
1993 – 1995	Patrick Ward, President and CEO of Caltex Petroleum
1995 – 1998	James Perrella, President and CEO of Ingersoll-Rand (a founding company)
1999 – 2001	Richard Swift, President and CEO of Foster Wheeler
2001 – 2004	Michael Jordan, CEO, EDS
2005 – 2007	Dinesh Paliwal, CEO, ABB North America
2008 - 2010	John Mullen, CEO, DHL Express
2011 –	Ambassador Alan Wolff, Senior Counsel, McKenna Long & Aldridge LLP

NFTC Presidents (1932-present)

1932 – 1950	Eugene P. Thomas
1950 – 1962	William S. Swingle
1962 – 1962	John Akin
1963 – 1979	Robert M. Norris
1979 – 1988	Richard W. Roberts
1988 – 2000	Frank Kittredge
2001 –	Bill Reinsch

APPENDIX B

Founding Members

Founding Members of the National Foreign Trade Council

In accordance with the first resolution of the first National Foreign Trade Convention, May 27-28, 1914, in Washington DC, the President of the Convention (Alba Johnson, President, Baldwin Locomotive) appointed the first members of the National Foreign Trade Council.

There were to be 30 founding members, with the option to increase membership at a later time.

The founding members of the NFTC were:

Chairman:
James A. Farrell, President, United States Steel Corporation, New York.

Sam D. Capen, President, Business Men's League, St. Louis Missouri.

J.A.G. Carson, Vice-President, Savannah Board of Trade, Savannah, Georgia.

E.A.S. Clarke, President, Lackawanna Steel Company, New York.

Walter L. Clark, Vice-President, Niles-Bement-Pond Company, New York.

Samuel P. Colt, President, United States Rubber Company, Providence.

Maurice Coster, Foreign Manager, Westinghouse Electric & Manufacturing Company, New York.

Robert Dollar, President, Robert Dollar Steamship Company, San Francisco.

John F. Fitzgerald, Chairman, Foreign Trade Committee, Boston Chamber of Commerce, Boston.

P.A.S. Franklin, Vice-President, International Mercantile Marine, New York.

Hon. Lloyd C. Griscom, New York.

Fairfaix Harrison, President, Southern Railway, Washington, D.C.

H.G. Herget, President, Illinois Manufacturers' Association, New York.

James J. Hill, Chairman of the Board, Great Northern Railway, St. Paul.

E.N. Hurley, President, Hurley Machine Company, Chicago.

Chas E. Jennings, President, American Manufacturers Export Association, New York.

Alba B. Johnson, President, Baldwin Locomotive Works, Philadelphia.

D.W. Kempner, Galveston Cotton Exchange, Galveston.

Cyrus H. McCormick, President, International Harvester Corporation, Chicago.

Barton Meyers, President, Chamber of Commerce, Norfolk.

Chas M. Muchnic, Foreign Manager, American Locomotive Company, New York.

A.H. Mulliken Jr., President, Pettibone-Mulliken Company, Chicago.

M.A. Oudin, Foreign Manager, General Electric Company, Schenectady, N.Y.

William Pigott, Vice-President, Seattle Car & Foundry Company, Seattle.

George M. Reynolds, President, Continental and Commercial Bank, Chicago

Welding Ring, Former President, New York Produce Exchange, New York.

John D. Ryan, President, Amalgamated Copper Company, New York.

W.L. Saunders, President, Ingersoll-Rand Company, New York.

Charles A. Schieren, Jr., President, Charles A. Schieren Company, New York.

W.D. Simmons, President, Simmons Hardware Company, St. Louis.

Ellison A. Smyth, President, Pelzer Cotton Mills, Greenville, S.C.

Willard Straight, President, American Asiatic Association, New York.

Stewart K. Taylor, Mobile Chamber of Commerce, Mobile.

E.P. Thomas, President, United States Steel Products Company, New York.

F.A. Vanderlip, President, National City Bank, New York.

Secretary: Robert H. Patchin, Manufacturers' Export Association, New York.

APPENDIX C

Member Companies of the 2014 NFTC Board of Directors, and Founding Members Still Active with the NFTC

Company, Year Joined the NFTC

ABB Incorporated, 1975

AbbVie Inc., 2013

Applied Materials, 1999

British American Tobacco Company, 2012

Baxter International, Incorporated, 2006

Caterpillar Incorporated, 1970

Chevron Corporation, 1972

Chrysler Corporation, 1971

CIGNA International Health Benefits, 1998

Cisco Systems, Inc., 2014

The Coca Cola Company, 1975

ConocoPhillips, Inc., 1999

Deloitte & Touche, 1999

DHL North America, 2008

eBay Inc., 2012

E.I. du Pont de Nemours & Company (DuPont), 1914*, rejoined 1971

Ernst & Young LLP, 1969

ExxonMobil Corporation, 1973

Fluor Corporation, 1999

Ford Motor Company, 1978

General Electric Company, 1914*, rejoined 1973

Google Inc., 2010

Halliburton Company, 1979

Hanesbrands Inc., 2006

Hercules Group, 2005

Hewlett-Packard Company, 1987

Johnson & Johnson, 1972

JPMorganChase & Co, 1975

KPMG LLP, 1972

Mars Incorporated, 1988

Mayer Brown, 2010

McCormick & Company, Inc., 2007

McKenna Long & Aldridge LLP, 2004

Microsoft Corporation, 1997

National Foreign Trade Council, 1914*

Occidental Petroleum Corporation, 1998

Oracle Corporation, 1998

Pernod Ricard USA, 2002

Pfizer International Incorporated, 1992

PricewaterhouseCoopers LLP, 2001

Procter & Gamble Company, 1974

Prudential Insurance Company, 1985

Ridgewood Group International, Limited, 1989

Siemens Corporation, 1981

Sullivan & Worcester LLP, 2004

TE Connectivity, 2007

Toyota Motor Sales, USA, Incorporated, 1981

Tyco International, 1998

United Parcel Service, Inc., 2009

United Technologies Corporation, 1979

Visa Inc., 2012

Wal-Mart Stores, Incorporated, 1994

*Founding members of the NFTC

In addition to the three Board Member companies indicated above,
three additional founding member companies remain active NFTC members
today, and deserve recognition here:

Citigroup Inc. (then National City Bank of New York), 1914*, rejoined 1972
Ingersoll Rand, 1914*, rejoined 1992
United States Steel Corporation, 1914*, rejoined 2012

APPENDIX D

Dollar Award and World Trade Award Recipients

Recipients of the Captain Robert Dollar Memorial Award

The Captain Robert Dollar Memorial Award was presented annually from 1938 to 1985 by the National Foreign Trade Council "for distinguished contribution to the advancement of American foreign trade and investment."

The award was established in 1937 by the Dollar Family of San Francisco in memory of Captain Robert Dollar, pioneer in American shipping and world trade, and a charter member of the National Foreign Trade Council.

Cordell Hull, Secretary of State	1938
James A. Farrell, National Foreign Trade Council	1939
Thomas J. Watson, IBM	1940
Eugene P. Thomas, National Foreign Trade Council	1941
Sumner Welles, US Undersecretary of State	1942
Juan T. Trippe, Pan American Airways	1943
Eric A. Johnston, US Chamber of Commerce	1944
Fred I Kent, Bankers Trust Company	1945
William L. Clayton, Undersecretary of State for Economic Affairs	1946
John Abbink, McGraw-Hill International	1947
Albert F. Loree, National Foreign Trade Council	1948
Christian A. Herter, US House of Representatives	1949
Paul G. Hoffman, Economic Cooperation Administration	1950
James A. Farley, Coca-Cola Export Corporation	1951

Edward Riley, General Motors	1952
Eugene Holman, Standard Oil	1953
Clarence B. Randall, Inland Steel	1954
George W. Wolf, United States Steel Export Co.	1955
William S. Swingle, National Foreign Trade Council	1956
Howard C. Sheperd, First National City Bank of New York	1957
W. Rogers Herod, International General Electric Co.	1958
Samuel C. Waugh, Export-Import Bank	1959
Henry W. Balgooyen, American & Foreign Power Co.	1960
J. Peter Grace, W. R. Grace & Co.	1961
William E. Knox, Westinghouse Electric International Co.	1962
James A. Farrell, Jr., Farrell Lines, Inc.	1963
David Rockefeller, Chase Manhattan Bank	1964
Thomas J. Watson, Jr., IBM	1965
George S. Moore, First National City Bank	1966
William Blackie, Caterpillar Tractor Co.	1967
Harold F. Linder, Export-Import Bank	1968
Elis S. Hoglund, National Foreign Trade Council	1969
Rudolph A. Peterson, Bank of America NT&SA	1970
Henry Kearns, Export-Import Bank	1971
Robert J. Dixson, Johnson & Johnson; National Foreign Trade Council	1972
Walter B. Wriston, First National City Corporation	1973
George P. Shultz, Bechtel Corporation	1974
Stephen D. Bechtel, Bechtel Group of Companies	1975
Reginald H. Jones, General Electric Co.	1976
Irving S. Shapiro, DuPont Co.	1977
J. Paul Austin, The Coca-Cola Company	1978
J. Robert Fluor, Fluor Corporation	1979
T.A. Wilson, The Boeing Co.	1980
A.W. Clausen, The World Bank	1981
William E. Brock, United States Trade Representative	1982
Malcolm Baldrige, US Secretary of Commerce	1983
Lee L. Morgan, Caterpillar Tractor Co.	1984
David Packard, Hewlett-Packard Co.	1985

Recipients of the NFTC World Trade Award

In February 2002, the Board of Directors of the NFTC reinstated an annual award in the tradition of the Captain Robert Dollar Memorial Award for lifetime achievement in advancing open world trade and investment.

Recipients of the NFTC World Trade Award -
"Reviving the spirit of the Captain Robert Dollar Memorial Award"

Donald Evans, US Secretary of Commerce	2002
Lee Raymond, ExxonMobil	2003
Raymond V. Gilmartin, Merck & Company	2004
Michael Jordan, EDS Corporation	2005
Charles O. Holliday, Jr DuPont Co.	2006
James W. Owens, Caterpillar, Inc.	2007
Gregory W. Meeks, U.S. House of Representatives	2008
Herbert L. Henkel, Ingersoll Rand	2009
Congressman Dave Camp, US House of Representatives	2010
Congressman David Dreier, US House of Representatives	2012
Dr. C. Fred Bergsten, Peterson Institute for International Economics	2013

APPENDIX E

Addresses of the NFTC

**NFTC Organizational
Addresses**

<u>New York City Offices</u>

1914-1915/1916
64 Stone Street
New York, NY

1915/1916-1948
India House
1 Hanover Square
New York, NY

1948-1962
111 Broadway
New York, NY

1962-1982
10 Rockefeller Plaza
New York, NY

1982-1992
100 East 42nd Street
New York, NY

1993-2001
1270 Avenue of the Americas
New York, NY

2001-2008/9
2 W 45th Street
New York, NY

2008/9-2011
600 Lexington Avenue
29th Floor
New York, NY

2011-2014
60 East 42nd Street
Suite 920
New York, NY

2014-
60 East 42nd Street
Suite 1136
New York, NY

<u>Washington, DC Offices</u>

1980-1983
1835 K Street NW
Washington DC

1983-1988
900 17th St NW
Washington DC

1988 -
1625 K Street NW
#200
Washington DC

Historic Timeline of the National Foreign Trade Council

National Foreign Trade Council Historic Timeline

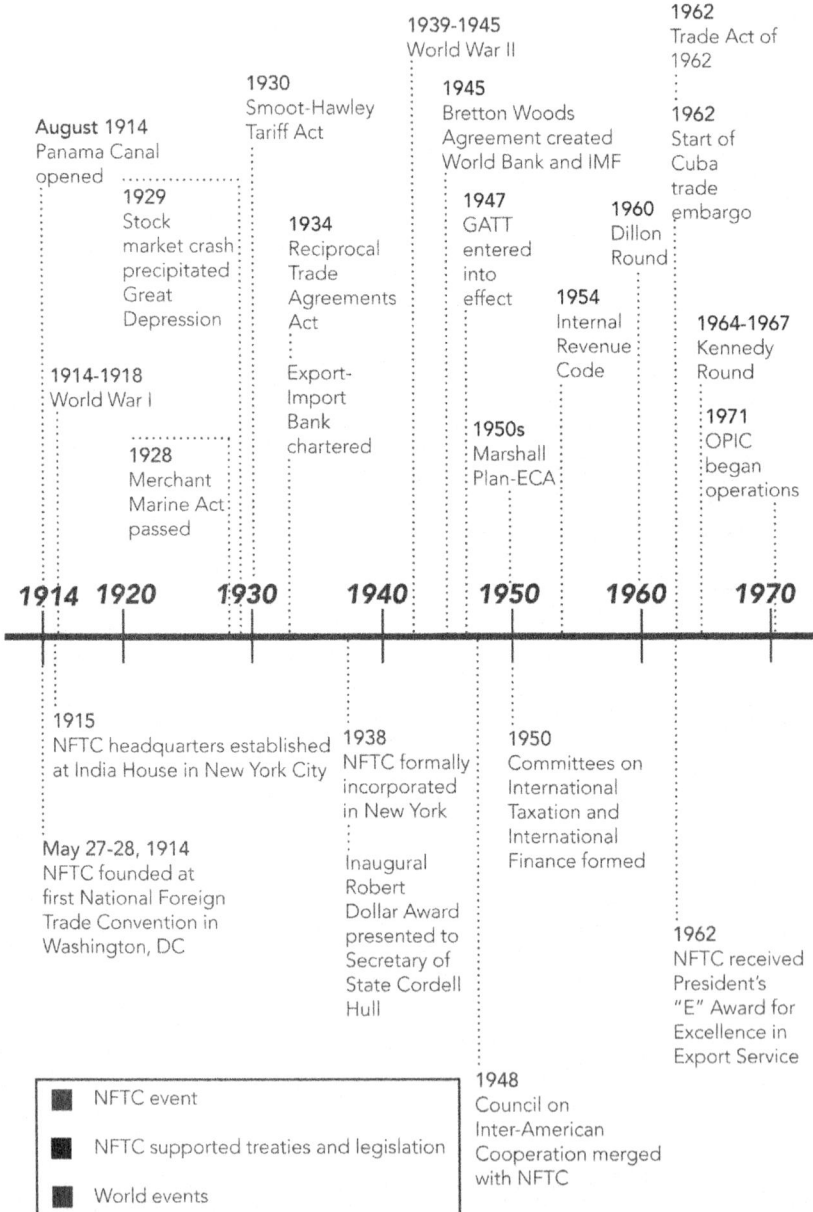

August 1914
Panama Canal opened

1914-1918
World War I

1929
Stock market crash precipitated Great Depression

1928
Merchant Marine Act passed

1930
Smoot-Hawley Tariff Act

1934
Reciprocal Trade Agreements Act

Export-Import Bank chartered

1939-1945
World War II

1945
Bretton Woods Agreement created World Bank and IMF

1947
GATT entered into effect

1950s
Marshall Plan-ECA

1954
Internal Revenue Code

1960
Dillon Round

1962
Trade Act of 1962

1962
Start of Cuba trade embargo

1964-1967
Kennedy Round

1971
OPIC began operations

1914   1920   1930   1940   1950   1960   1970

1915
NFTC headquarters established at India House in New York City

May 27-28, 1914
NFTC founded at first National Foreign Trade Convention in Washington, DC

1938
NFTC formally incorporated in New York

Inaugural Robert Dollar Award presented to Secretary of State Cordell Hull

1950
Committees on International Taxation and International Finance formed

1962
NFTC received President's "E" Award for Excellence in Export Service

1948
Council on Inter-American Cooperation merged with NFTC

- ▦ NFTC event
- ▦ NFTC supported treaties and legislation
- ▦ World events

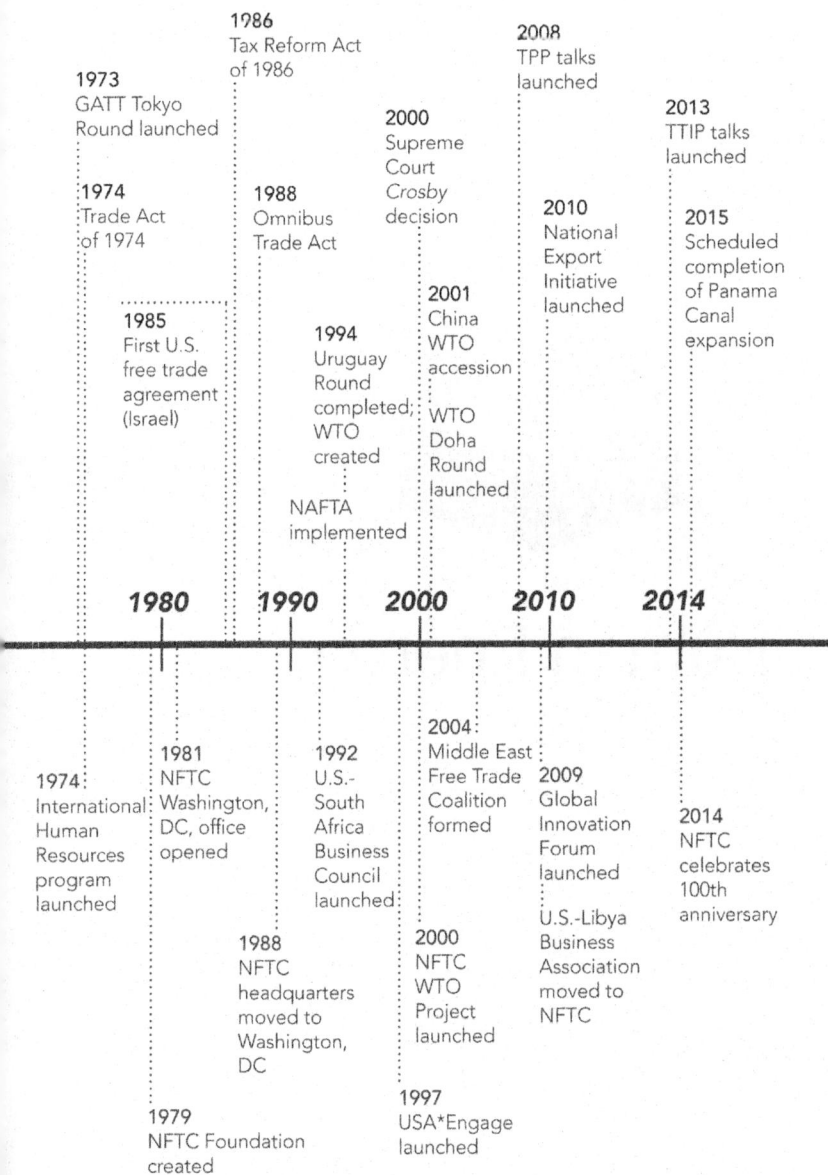

1973
GATT Tokyo
Round launched

1974
Trade Act
of 1974

1985
First U.S.
free trade
agreement
(Israel)

1986
Tax Reform Act
of 1986

1988
Omnibus
Trade Act

1994
Uruguay
Round
completed;
WTO
created

NAFTA
implemented

2000
Supreme
Court
Crosby
decision

2001
China
WTO
accession

WTO
Doha
Round
launched

2008
TPP talks
launched

2010
National
Export
Initiative
launched

2013
TTIP talks
launched

2015
Scheduled
completion
of Panama
Canal
expansion

1980   **1990**   **2000**   **2010**   **2014**

1974
International
Human
Resources
program
launched

1981
NFTC
Washington,
DC, office
opened

1979
NFTC Foundation
created

1988
NFTC
headquarters
moved to
Washington,
DC

1992
U.S.-
South
Africa
Business
Council
launched

2004
Middle East
Free Trade
Coalition
formed

2000
NFTC
WTO
Project
launched

1997
USA*Engage
launched

2009
Global
Innovation
Forum
launched

U.S.-Libya
Business
Association
moved to
NFTC

2014
NFTC
celebrates
100th
anniversary

**Chevron
Joined 1972**

ExxonMobil

ExxonMobil
Joined 1973

KPMG
Joined 1972

Google™

Google
Joined 2010

TOYOTA

Toyota
Joined 1981

Visa
Joined 2012

Citigroup
Joined 1914

DHL
Joined 2008

Building a better
working world

Ernst and Young
Joined 1969

MARS incorporated

Mars Incorporated
Joined 1988

P&G

Procter and Gamble
Joined 1974

PHILIP MORRIS INTERNATIONAL

PMI Global Services Inc.
Joined 1973

SIEMENS

Siemens
Joined 1981

TE connectivity

TE Connectivity
Joined 2007

NFTC Centennial Silver Sponsors

ABB Inc., 1975

Amgen, 2013

Caterpillar Inc., 1970

Chubb

The Coca Cola Company, 1975

E.I. DuPont de Nemours and Company (Dupont), 1914; rejoined 1971

Ford Motor Company, 1978

HP, 1997

Korea International Trade Association (KITA)

McKenna Long & Aldridge LLP, 2004

Pernod Ricard USA, 2002

Tyco International, 1998

Walmart Stores, Inc., 1994

INDEX

CPSIA information can be obtained at www.ICGtesting.com
Printed in the USA
BVOW09s1918171114

375511BV00004B/9/P